Gross State Product and Productivity in the Southeast provides the most thorough analysis of southeastern economic growth to date. In the past, state and regional economic analysis has been hampered by the absence of available statistical information. This comparison of the economic growth in the Southeast with that in the United States between 1950 and 1970 presents data that can be extended by those who wish to project the economic growth of the region, or of the specific states that compose it, beyond 1970.

The analysis of growth in this study is conducted through the preparation and presentation of gross state product figures for each southeastern state and gross regional product figures for the Southeast. The concept of gross state (regional) product and the estimation procedure followed to develop the gross state (regional) product estimates are carefully explained in the text. A detailed appendix contains estimates of gross product for the Southeast and for each of the southeastern states; the estimates are provided for each year during the 1950-70 period and are disaggregated according to the one-digit major industry groups. Real output growth, industrial

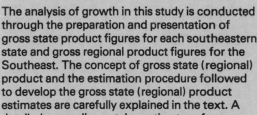

(continued on back flap)

output trends, and labor-
re examined for each state,
on-Southeast, and the
eastern growth performance is compared to national and non-southeastern performance, and it is shown that in most phases of economic growth the Southeast has outperformed the rest of the United States. The author provides a full examination of state and industry sources of recent southeastern expansion and closes with an assessment of the causal factors underlying the recent surge of economic activity in the Southeast.

The appendix tables contain a rich data base for those engaged in research of the southeastern economy, scholars interested in state and regional economics and businessmen who have a particular interest in the Southeast.

Albert W. Niemi, Jr., associate professor of economics at the University of Georgia, is a regular contributor to the business and economics journals and is author of State and Regional Patterns in American Manufacturing, 1860-1900.

Gross State Product and
Productivity in the Southeast

Gross State Product and Productivity in the Southeast

by Albert W. Niemi, Jr.

The University of North Carolina Press
Chapel Hill

Library of Congress Cataloging in Publication Data

Niemi, Albert W
    Gross state product and productivity in the Southeast

    Bibliography: p.
    1. Gross national product—Southern States.
1. Title.
HC107.A1331516   339.375   74-14923
ISBN 0-8078-1238-2

For my sons, Bert and Eddie

Contents

List of Tables

List of Appendix Tables

Preface

During the past several decades, the Southeast has been experiencing a rapid economic expansion. However, at present, there are no readily available aggregate data series that allow for accurate measurement of the dimensions and sources of this recent prosperity. As a basis for gauging the nature and degree of recent southeastern expansion, I have provided estimates of gross state product, by major industry, for each of the southeastern states and gross regional product for the Southeast region. Conceptually, gross state product and gross regional product are the state and regional equivalent of gross national product; the figures represent the total output produced in an area during a given accounting period.

Chapter I provides a full discussion of the concept of gross state product and explains the estimation procedure followed in this study. Chapters II and III examine growth trends during 1950-70 in the United States, the Southeast region, and the individual southeastern states. Chapter IV examines per capita output trends and is directed at a discussion of the issue of southeastern convergence to national per capita output standards. Chapter V provides an analysis of the impact of productivity advance on recent southeastern economic growth and compares this with national developments. Chapter VI concludes with an assessment of the factors that have been reponsible for the postwar economic expansion of the Southeast. A lengthy statistical appendix is also included, and it is hoped that the estimates provided in this study will stimulate and encourage further research into state and regional economic growth. The data bank supplied in this work represents an invaluable research aid to those concerned with the southeastern economy. The historical gross state product series provides a convenient base to which gross state product estimates for later periods can be added. Efforts at gross state product estimation are currently underway in many states, and, as these results become available, additional analyses will become possible.

The concept of gross state product was developed by John W.

Kendrick. As a graduate student at the University of Connecticut, I worked as Dr. Kendrick's research assistant in the preparation of gross state product estimates for the New England states. In this process, I gained considerable knowledge and insight into the data problems involved in state and regional economic analysis. In the preparation of this manuscript, I have relied on Dr. Kendrick for advice and comments. He has been a continuous source of wisdom and encouragement, and my debt to him is very great.

I am also indebted to the late Dr. William B. Keeling, director of the Division of Research, College of Business Administration, University of Georgia. His assistance, advice, and encouragement were instrumental in the planning and preparation of this manuscript.

Special thanks go to the College of Business Administration for providing me with the time, secretarial assistance, and atmosphere conducive to the completion of this work. I am also grateful to my research assistant, Christopher Catledge, who computed many of the estimates. Finally, I am indebted to my wife, Maria, who provided a careful reading of the entire manuscript and made many valuable suggestions.

Gross State Product and
Productivity in the Southeast

I. The Concept and Estimation of Gross State Product

For the past two decades the Southeast has experienced a period of relatively high economic growth. [1] The purpose of this study is, first, to analyze the dimensions of this growth and its industrial origins and, second, to compare the growth performance of the Southeast and the individual southeastern states with the performance of the nation as a whole. The method employed in this study is to examine southeastern economic growth through the preparation and presentation of gross state product estimates for the southeastern states and gross regional product estimates for the Southeast region as a whole.

In recent years, there has been a lack of any comprehensive aggregate economic data available at the state or regional level; thus, it has been necessary to estimate gross state product. Gross state product is the only measure that adequately reflects a state's or region's aggregate production, and, therefore, it is an essential measure for studying economic growth at the state or regional level. However, gross state product figures for the individual states are not readily available, and a careful and arduous procedure must be followed in order to prepare accurate estimates of state and regional product. At present, the only aggregate measure of economic activity available on a state or regional basis is personal income, published by the U.S. Department of Commerce; however, this series does not accurately reflect productive economic activity but rather indicates income received by persons in an area. [2] Personal income is useful in studying consumption patterns, but it can be misleading in evaluating economic performance; in fact, secular and cyclical fluctuations in personal income deviate significantly from those in gross product.

CONCEPT OF GROSS STATE PRODUCT

Gross state product represents the total economic activity of a state in the same manner that gross national product (G.N.P.) represents the total economic activity of the nation; gross regional product is simply

3

the regional equivalent to gross state product. Gross state product can be defined as the sum of the value of all goods produced for final sale in an accounting period. Alternatively, it can be defined as the sum of the total market value of all output minus the value of intermediate production expenses. Despite these similarities, there is one minor conceptual difference between gross state product and G.N.P. Gross state product is defined on a geographic basis; it represents the sum of output originating as a result of labor, capital, and other factors applied in the area in question, regardless of the residence of those factors. An adjustment, net income from abroad, is made in the calculations of G.N.P. In this adjustment, income earned by American factors of production abroad is added to G.N.P., and income earned by foreign factors of production in the United States is deducted from G.N.P. An alternative accounting concept, gross domestic product, includes output regardless of residence and is more strictly in conformity with the concept of gross state product. However, since gross domestic product and G.N.P. are virtually the same, and since G.N.P. is the accepted accounting concept in the United States, comparisons have been made with the latter.

APPROACHES TO ESTIMATION OF GROSS STATE PRODUCT

Theoretically, there are several alternative approaches to the estimation of gross product. The procedure used in this study was developed by John W. Kendrick and C. Milton Jaycox and involves the estimation of value added by major industry. [3] Gross product originating is estimated separately for each of the major industries and summed to yield gross state product. This approach is desirable since it provides an industry disaggregation of gross state product, which is then useful in analyzing the industrial composition of state or regional economic growth. Another advantage of the value added by industry approach is that it permits use of available national industry deflators, and, therefore, it yields a more exact and simple deflation procedure. Due to the lack of available state and regional price statistics, alternative procedures for estimating gross state product must resort to a single aggregate gross state product deflator. Another advantage of the value added by industry approach is that the gross state product figure is provided in a form that is readily adaptable to productivity analysis. The Kendrick-Jaycox method was used by this author to estimate gross state product for Georgia and the New England states, and variants of the Kendrick-Jaycox technique have been used to estimate gross state product for Ohio, Louisiana, South Dakota, Idaho, Washington, and Oregon. [4]

Two additional approaches are common in the estimation of gross product originating: the expenditure approach and the income approach. The gross expenditure approach involves the summation of the major categories of spending for a given accounting period. This is generally represented by the following identity:

$$Y = C + I + G + \text{Net } X$$

where C = consumption, I = investment, G = government expenditures, and Net X = net exports. Due to the difficulty involved in measuring net exports across state and regional boundaries, the expenditure approach is not generally feasible for gross state product estimation. [5] Recent work at the Harvard Economic Research Project by Karen Polenske, Raymond Scheppach, and John Rodgers has approached gross state product estimation from the expenditure side, and state estimates and projections were made for the following expenditure components: personal consumption, gross private domestic investment, gross exports, state and local government purchases, and federal government purchases. [6]

The income approach involves the summation of the various income flows that compose factor income: labor compensation, proprietors' income, net interest, rents, royalties, and corporate profits. Indirect business taxes, capital consumption allowances, and business transfer payments less subsidies are added to this sum of factor income to yield total gross income. The gross state product measure calculated as the sum of total gross income would not be available on a component breakdown that would be particularly useful for comparative state and regional economic analysis, and it would be difficult to develop an adequate deflation procedure.

An income approach to gross state product estimation recently was developed by Harold K. Charlesworth and William G. Herzel. [7] Their method employed the Commerce Department's personal income series and attempted to add to this the state estimates of corporate profits, capital consumption allowances, and indirect business taxes. Before deriving the estimates, all corporations were divided into two groups: firms doing business only in Kentucky and multistate firms; each of these categories was subdivided into manufacturing and nonmanufacturing firms.

The Charlesworth-Herzel approach is carefully developed and well documented but suffers from several problems, most of which reflect the handling of the multistate firms. Various rationing methods were developed to allocate a portion of the multistate firm's capital consumption allowances, indirect business taxes, and corporate profits to the state of Kentucky. The capital consumption allowances were allocated simply by computing the percentage share of a corporation's property existing in a particular state and depreciating this on the basis of the allowances claimed on the corporate income tax returns. Many of the indirect business taxes were documented by returns and little problem was encountered in their allocation. There was some difficulty in assigning federal excise taxes and other indirect business taxes, and the authors decided to allocate these according to where the product was produced. Corporate profits were distributed according to the state's share of the firm's total labor payroll.

The Charlesworth-Herzel approach attempted to circumvent the assumption of similarity in factor proportions between the nation and the individual states which is implicit in the value added by industry approach used in this study.[8] However, Charlesworth and Herzel arrived at the position of distributing significant portions of the non-labor shares of output according to labor payroll shares: it will be shown below that this is exactly what the method employed in this study assumes. However, this author's method makes the assumption of similar factor proportions for individual industries rather than for two broad categories of economic activity, manufacturing and non-manufacturing. The Charlesworth-Herzel method also fails to provide the gross state product figure in a form conducive to many interesting state and regional analyses, and it is very difficult to develop a workable deflation procedure.[9]

J. Thomas Romans provided estimates of gross state product derived from a procedure involving the income-product identity.[10] He defined gross state income (GSY) as follows:

$$GSY = C + I + G + \text{Net X}$$

or alternatively

$$GSY = C + S + T_n$$

where S = savings, T_n = taxes net of government transfers, and all other symbols are as before. Romans attempted to directly estimate savings and taxes net of government transfers. After savings were estimated, consumption was estimated as the difference between disposable personal income and savings. The major problems involved in Romans's procedure are that the major portion of gross state product is derived as a residual, and it is difficult to deflate the gross state product figure.

Detailed sets of integrated economic accounts have been prepared for Hawaii, Illinois, Iowa, and Arkansas. [11] The pioneering work in this area was done by Harry Oshima and his associates at the University of Hawaii. Oshima's group prepared gross state product estimates using both the income and product approaches. On the income side, they provided the following disaggregation: labor income, employer's contributions for social insurance, income of unincorporated enterprises, rental income, dividends, net interest, undistributed profits, corporate taxes, indirect business taxes, business transfer payments, and depreciation allowances. On the expenditure side, they provided the following disaggregation: personal consumption expenditures, government purchase of goods and services, investment (construction, plant and equipment, and change in inventories), and net exports of goods and services. They also provided a detailed summary for the household account, local government account, savings-investment account, federal agencies account, and external account.

Gross state product estimates have also resulted as by-products of state input-output studies. Following the pioneering work of Walter Isard, Frederick Moore, and James Petersen, there have been numerous attempts to prepare input-output tables for state economies. [12] In recent years, input-output studies have been completed for the following states: Maryland, West Virginia, South Carolina, Georgia, Kentucky, Tennessee, Mississippi, Missouri, Kansas, Oklahoma, Texas, New Mexico, Arizona, Utah, Idaho, Oregon, and Washington. [13] Criticism of state input-output models has centered on the assumption of similar production functions in all states and the nation and the difficulty in measuring net exports. [14]

USES OF GROSS STATE PRODUCT ESTIMATES

Gross state product estimates, calculated on a major industry breakdown, provide a convenient basis for analyzing aggregate economic growth, per capita output performance, structural changes in the composition of an economy, and productivity trends. Estimates provided for a group of states permit a comparison of state growth trends within the region. Since the gross state product estimates are conceptually equivalent to G.N.P., it is also possible to develop comparisons among state, regional, and national growth trends. The gross state product estimates are necessary in order to forecast future growth, and the resulting projections should be useful to federal, state, and local governmental agencies as well as to businesses operating within the particular state. [15]

RECENT INTEREST IN GROSS STATE PRODUCT ESTIMATION

There is a great deal of current interest in gross state product estimation, particularly in the Southeast. In addition to this author's work and the work of Charlesworth and Herzel, efforts are underway to estimate gross state product in Tennessee, Mississippi, and Florida. Recent meetings of the Southern Economic Association and Southeast Income Conference have devoted sessions to the issue of gross state product estimation. A portion of the meeting at the Southern Economic Association was highlighted in a recent issue of *Growth and Change*, and a strong case was made for additional state and regional data, especially a gross state product series. [16]

The Bank of California has developed current dollar-aggregate gross state product estimates for all states for several bench-mark years. The University of California at Los Angeles and the University of Pennsylvania have been involved in developing state econometric models, and, in several instances, gross state product estimates have been generated as a by-product of this work. [17] The econometric-model approach has also been used by Harold Moody, Frank Puffer, and Robert Williams to generate gross regional product estimates for eight United States regions. [18] The recent work by the Harvard Economic Research Project has resulted in estimates and projections of gross output and employment for all states. [19] In addition to these ongoing and completed projects concerning gross state product estimation, there are numerous projects, still in the formative stages, that have equally ambitious goals.

In the past, state and regional economic analysis has been hampered by data limitations. However, recent theoretical models and computer technology have made possible the estimation and presentation of gross state product figures at a modest cost. The development of a gross state product series is essential if we are to further our knowledge and understanding of state and regional economic growth.

ESTIMATION PROCEDURE: CURRENT DOLLAR ESTIMATES

As indicated earlier, the basic method used in this study was developed by John Kendrick and Milton Jaycox. Some modification has been introduced in the procedure for estimating gross manufacturing product, and this will be explained below. The Kendrick-Jaycox approach involves estimating value added by major industry, and the estimation is conducted on the following component breakdown:

> Government
> Farm
> Private Nonfarm
>> Mining
>> Construction
>> Manufacturing
>> Trade
>> Finance, Insurance, and Real Estate
>> Transportation, Communication, and
>>> Public Utilities
>> Services and Other

Gross product originating is estimated separately for each of the major industry categories.

In the government sector, the procedure follows the Department of Commerce concept of gross government product, defined as the compensation of general government employees. This involves summing wages and salaries plus supplements. The wage and salary portion represents more than 90% of gross government product, and this is available on a state basis in the Commerce Department's personal income series. The supplement portion of gross government product is estimated by applying the national ratio of supplements to wages and salaries for each year to the state government wage and salary figures. [20]

The estimates of gross farm product are computed entirely from data published by the U.S. Department of Agriculture. The annual supplement to the July issue of the *Farm Income Situation* provides all the data needed to estimate gross farm product. [21] (See table 1 for an example of the estimation procedure for North Carolina in 1970.)

TABLE 1

GROSS FARM PRODUCT OF NORTH CAROLINA, 1970

Item	Millions of Dollars
Value of Total Farm Output	
1. Cash receipts from marketing	$1543.9
2. Value of home consumption	51.9
3. Gross rental value of dwellings	95.9
4. Net rent to nonfarm landlords	42.0
5. Net change in inventories	6.1
6. Total (1+2+3-4+5)	1655.8
Intermediate Production Expenses	
7. Feed	215.2
8. Livestock	42.7
9. Seed	16.1
10. Fertilizer	70.2
11. Repair and operation of equipment	148.2
12. Miscellaneous operating expenses	121.0
13. Total (7+8+9+10+11+12)	613.4
Gross Farm Product (6-13)	1042.4

Source: See text.

An identical procedure is followed for all industries in the private nonfarm sector. The technique involves the application of a series of national coefficients to available state data and estimated state totals. The procedure followed for the private nonfarm industries was made possible by the Commerce Department's development of estimates of G.N.P. by major industry. [22] The foundation for the gross state product estimate for the private nonfarm industries is income received by persons for participation in current production. Income received is defined to include wage and salary disbursements, other labor income, and proprietors' income. In contrast to personal income, it does not include transfer payments, rental income, interest, and dividends. [23]

The national ratio of income originating to income received is used in order to obtain state income originating estimates by industry for given years. A similar utilization of national coefficients is made in estimating capital consumption allowances and indirect business taxes for each industry for each year. The procedure for a given year for a particular industry (a) can be represented as follows:

$$\frac{YO_n^a}{YR_n^a} \cdot YR_s^a = YO_s^a$$

$$\frac{KC_n^a}{YO_n^a} \cdot YO_s^a = KC_s^a$$

$$\frac{IBT_n^a}{YO_n^a} \cdot YO_s^a = IBT_s^a$$

where YO = income originating, YR = income received, KC = capital consumption allowances, IBT = indirect business taxes, a represents industry a, and the subscripts n and s represent nation and state respectively. [24] The three components are summed:

$$YO_s^a + KC_s^a + IBT_s^a = GPO_s^a$$

where GPO_s^a = gross product originating in industry a for the particular state. Summing the product originating figures for the various industries for a state in a given year yields gross state product. (See exhibit A for a sample worksheet used to construct gross product originating in the private nonfarm industries.) [25]

The estimate of gross product originating in manufacturing yielded by the above procedure is adjusted to better reflect the peculiarities of the individual states. John Kendrick developed the adjustment procedure and suggested it to this author. As outlined above, the statistical basis of the gross state product estimate is a payroll figure, income received. For each private nonfarm industry, gross product originating is estimated on the basis of the national ratio of output to payroll; this is what is assumed in the use of national coefficients to inflate income received into gross product. In other words, the Kendrick-Jaycox procedure involves the assumption that within given private nonfarm industries, factor proportions (output/labor ratios) are similar in the nation and in the particular state. Further examination of the legitimacy of this assumption is investigated later in this chapter. The purpose of adjusting the estimate of gross product originating in manufacturing is to eliminate any bias introduced by this assumption of similar factor proportions. State manufacturing value added and labor payroll data, published by the Commerce Department in the *Annual Survey of Manufactures*, serve as the foundation for the adjustment factor. [26] Value added per dollar of labor

EXHIBIT A

SAMPLE WORKSHEET FOR ESTIMATING CURRENT DOLLAR GROSS PRODUCT ORIGINATING IN THE PRIVATE

NONFARM INDUSTRIES, NORTH CAROLINA, 1970

| | National Coefficients[a] | | | | North Carolina Data and Estimates (Millions of Dollars) | | | |
| | (a) | (b) | (c) | (d) | (e) | (f) | (g) | (h) |
Economic Sector	YO/YR	KC/YO	IBT/YO	YR	YO (a x d)	KC (b x e)	IBT (c x e)	GPO (e + f + g)
Mining	1.132	.511	.189	28	31.7	16.2	6.0	53.9
Construction	1.086	.062	.031	740	803.6	49.8	24.9	878.3
Manufacturing	1.237	.101	.087	4632	5729.8	578.7	498.5	6807.0
Trade	1.157	.070	.286	2093	2421.6	169.5	692.6	3283.7
Finance, Insurance and Real Estate	2.621	.245	.296	555	1454.7	356.4	430.6	2241.7
Transportation, Communication and Public Utilities	1.354	.234	.145	784	1061.5	248.4	153.9	1463.8
Services	1.098	.081	.027	1622	1781.0	144.3	48.1	1973.4

[a]The following symbols are used in the table heading: YO = income originating, YR = income received, KC = capital consumption, IBT = indirect business taxes, and GPO = gross product originating.

Source: See text.

payroll in the state is compared to value added per dollar of labor payroll in the nation as follows:

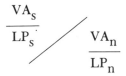

$$\frac{VA_s}{LP_s} \bigg/ \frac{VA_n}{LP_n}$$

where VA = value added, LP = dollars allocated to labor payroll, and the subscripts s and n refer to state and nation respectively. The product of this ratio times the unadjusted estimate of state gross product originating in manufacturing yields an adjusted estimate of gross manufacturing product.[27]

ESTIMATION PROCEDURE: CONSTANT DOLLAR ESTIMATES

Estimates of constant dollar gross product in the private nonfarm industries are prepared by directly using the national implicit industry deflators, defined as the ratio of current-dollar product to constant-dollar product, available from the Department of Commerce.[28] It can be argued that this deflation procedure provides an adequate method of calculating real gross state product since the industry weights in each state are determined apart from the deflation procedure. In the farm sector the double deflation approach is followed. The individual components of production expenses are deflated by the use of national deflators for these various items. National indexes of average prices received by farmers are used to deflate the value of total output. The difference between the two deflated totals, real value of total output minus real production expenses, yields real gross farm product. [29]

The procedure followed to deflate gross government product is that prescribed by the Commerce Department. This involves using average compensation per government employee to deflate as follows:

$$GGP \quad \frac{N_g}{LP_g} = \frac{GGP}{P}$$

where GGP = gross government product in current dollars, N_g = government employment, LP_g = compensation of government employees, and GGP/P = real gross government product. Since gross government product is estimated as the sum of government-employee compensation, real government output is assumed to parallel changes in government employment. Therefore, productivity analysis is not possible in the government sector since changes in output and employment are parallel and productivity is constant.

DIRECTNESS OF ESTIMATION

The modified version of the Kendrick-Jaycox method being used here encompasses direct estimates of gross farm product, government wages and salaries, and income received in the private nonfarm sector. In addition, the manufacturing adjustment attempts to eliminate any bias resulting from the use of national coefficients, and this is considered as justification for claiming directness in estimating gross product originating in manufacturing. Table 2 provides an example of the degree of direct estimation for North Carolina in 1970.

It is evident that the major portion of the gross state product figure results from direct estimation, although a considerable share remains for estimation by the Kendrick-Jaycox procedure of using national coefficients to inflate state income received data. The estimates resulting from the use of the Kendrick-Jaycox method should be viewed in the same light in which Kendrick and Jaycox originally viewed their contribution. They argued that the procedure was legitimate for providing estimates of state and regional product that could serve as the basis for analysis of state and regional growth trends.

TABLE 2

DIRECTNESS OF ESTIMATION OF GROSS STATE PRODUCT,

NORTH CAROLINA, 1970

Item	Millions of Dollars	% of Total
Direct Estimates		
Gross farm product	$ 1042.4	4.5
Government wages and salaries	2373.0	10.3
Income received in the private nonfarm industries less manufacturing	5822.0	25.1
Gross manufacturing product	7834.9	33.8
Total Direct Estimates	17072.3	73.7
Total Gross State Product	23164.1	

Source: See text.

CONSEQUENCES OF USING NATIONAL COEFFICIENTS

As noted above, the Kendrick-Jaycox method involves the assumption that within given major industries factor proportions are similar. The modified version of the Kendrick-Jaycox method used in this study attempts to get away from this assumption in manufacturing by adjusting for possible differences in the output/labor ratio. In a recent paper, I examined the appropriateness of the assumption that within manufacturing factor proportions were similar in all states. [30] My test results suggested that there were sufficient differences between states in factor proportions to warrant caution in this assumption. However, due to data limitations, my analysis was restricted to the manufacturing sector, and the value-added/labor-payroll weight devised by Kendrick can correct for this bias in manufacturing. The bias resulting from the assumption of similar factor proportions is likely to be much lower in those industries with high relative-labor inputs and those industries producing services; the nonmanufacturing private nonfarm industries generally fall into one of these two categories. I concluded my test of the Kendrick-Jaycox method by asserting that the modified Kendrick-Jaycox method, as applied in this study, can yield useful results for the state or regional economic analyst. However, an awareness of the limitations and biases incorporated in gross state product estimation is essential in order to interpret the significance of the results.

II. Economic Growth in the Southeast during 1950-1970

This chapter compares the 1950-70 economic performance in the Southeast with performance in the nation and in the non-Southeast. For the two-decade period, attention is focused on developments in the growth of real output, in the advancement of productivity, in changes in the structural composition of output, and in per capita performance. The analysis reveals that the Southeast has been in a period of high relative growth compared to national performance, and this strong relative growth performance has brought the region close to parity with national per capita output levels.

GROWTH IN REAL OUTPUT

For the past several decades, economic growth in the southeastern region has occurred at a significantly faster rate than growth in the rest of the economy. The Southeast's real (1958 dollars) gross regional product advanced at an average annual percentage rate of 4.6% and increased from $52.4 billion in 1950 to $129.9 billion in 1970. (See appendix tables I and II for current and constant-dollar estimates of gross regional product.) During this same period, the growth rate in real gross product was 3.6% in the nation and 3.4% outside the Southeast. Southeastern economic growth has been broadly based, and high growth rates in real output have been achieved in most industries, especially finance, insurance, and real estate (5.6%), transportation, communication, and public utilities (5.5%), and manufacturing (5.3%). In all industries except mining, the Southeast's growth performance substantially exceeded growth in the rest of the nation. (See table 3.)

A disaggregation of growth performance is provided in table 4 where decennial rates of change in real output are exhibited for 1950-60 and 1960-70. During the decade 1950-60, the Southeast ex-

TABLE 3

AVERAGE ANNUAL PERCENTAGE RATES OF CHANGE IN REAL

PRODUCT, UNITED STATES AND SOUTHEAST, 1950-70

Economic Sector	United States	Southeast	Non-Southeast
Private Nonfarm	3.8%	4.9%	3.5%
Mining	2.4	2.3	2.4
Construction	1.9	2.9	1.7
Manufacturing	3.7	5.3	3.4
Trade	3.8	4.8	3.6
Finance, Insurance and			
Real Estate	4.3	5.6	4.1
Transportation, Communication			
and Public Utilities	4.7	5.5	4.6
Services	3.9	4.4	3.6
Government	3.4	4.2	3.2
Farm	1.3	1.5	1.2
Total	3.6	4.6	3.4

Source: See text.

ceeded national growth in all industries except mining; during the decade 1960-70, the Southeast exceeded national growth in all industries. Both the non-Southeast and the Southeast experienced more rapid growth during the 1960s than during the 1950s; however, compared to the rest of the nation, southeastern growth was relatively greater during the decade of the sixties. The decennial rates of increase in real output in the fifties were 35.8% in the non-Southeast and 45.5% in the Southeast; the decennial rates of increase during the sixties were respectively 44.0% and 70.2%. The most marked relative advance for the Southeast during 1960-70 occurred in manufacturing; the region's growth rate more than doubled the average for the rest of the nation.

CHANGES IN THE STRUCTURAL COMPOSITION OF OUTPUT

The industrial composition of real output in the non-Southeast and the Southeast is shown in table 5. It is apparent from the figures that there is a great degree of similarity between the structure of the southeastern economy and the national economy. Slight differences in industrial structure existed in the period immediately following World War II, but during the past two decades these differences have virtually disappeared. Heavy emphasis in both economies is placed on manufacturing; approximately 30% of total output origi-

TABLE 4

DECENNIAL RATES OF CHANGE IN REAL PRODUCT, UNITED STATES

AND SOUTHEAST, 1950-60 AND 1960-70

Economic Sector	United States		Southeast		Non-Southeast	
	1950-60	1960-70	1950-60	1960-70	1950-60	1960-70
Private Nonfarm	38.9	51.9	48.2	76.8	37.4	46.1
Mining	22.4	31.3	8.4	47.2	26.2	28.3
Construction	34.0	8.8	40.5	26.7	32.6	5.5
Manufacturing	33.6	54.6	40.3	100.8	32.6	46.9
Trade	36.3	54.1	47.3	74.1	34.3	50.5
Finance, Insurance and Real Estate	56.3	49.1	83.1	62.8	52.5	46.9
Transportation, Communication and Public Utilities	45.8	72.4	56.1	88.7	44.3	69.1
Services	42.4	48.4	52.9	55.1	39.0	45.7
Government	37.0	42.3	46.0	57.0	34.9	38.9
Farm	13.2	13.0	18.7	13.3	11.7	13.3
Total	37.3	49.1	45.5	70.2	35.8	44.0

Source: See text.

nates in this industry. The high growth rate in southeastern manu-facturing is evidenced by a rise from 27.2% of gross regional product in 1950 to 30.9% in 1970. On the other hand, the slow growth rate in agriculture resulted in a decline from 8.0% of gross regional product in 1950 to 4.3% in 1970. In addition to the relative advance of manu-facturing in the Southeast, sharp relative increases were shown in finance, insurance, real estate, transportation, communication, and public utilities.

The Southeast's percentage shares of national output, by major industry, are shown in table 6, and it is clear from the figures that the Southeast experienced a significant increase in its industry shares, especially during the 1960s. During the period 1950-70, the sharpest increases occurred in manufacturing (13.5% to 18.4%), trade (14.1% to 17.3%), finance, insurance, and real estate (11.8% to 15.1%), and government (17.9% to 21.0%). The relative advance in manufacturing was especially rapid during the period 1960-70, increasing from 14.2% to 18.4%. The picture revealed by table 6 is one of strong relative-growth performance for the Southeast during the past two decades. It is evident from these figures that the South-east's growth has been broadly based and has involved heavy contri-butions to national production in all industries. In 1970, the region's shares of national production ranged from 15% in finance, insurance, and real estate to 21 % in mining, government, and agriculture.

TABLE 5

PERCENTAGE DISTRIBUTION OF REAL PRODUCT, NON-SOUTHEAST

AND SOUTHEAST, 1950, 1960, AND 1970

Economic Sector	Non-Southeast			Southeast		
	1950	1960	1970	1950	1960	1970
Mining	2.8%	2.6%	2.3%	4.4%	3.2%	2.8%
Construction	4.6	4.5	3.2	4.6	4.5	3.3
Manufacturing	30.2	29.6	29.9	27.2	26.2	30.9
Trade	17.2	17.0	17.7	16.3	16.5	16.9
Finance, Insurance and Real Estate	12.0	13.5	13.7	9.2	11.6	11.1
Transportation, Communication and Public Utilities	8.7	9.2	10.8	8.7	9.4	10.4
Services	9.3	9.5	9.6	9.3	9.8	8.9
Government	9.8	9.7	9.3	12.3	12.3	11.4
Farm	5.4	4.4	3.5	8.0	6.5	4.3

Source: See text.

TABLE 6

SOUTHEAST'S PERCENTAGE SHARES OF NATIONAL PRODUCT,

1950, 1960, AND 1970

Economic Sector	1950	1960	1970
Mining	21.3%	18.9%	21.2%
Construction	15.0	15.8	18.4
Manufacturing	13.5	14.2	18.4
Trade	14.1	15.3	17.3
Finance, Insurance and Real Estate	11.8	13.8	15.1
Transportation, Communication and Public Utilities	14.9	15.9	17.4
Services	14.2	15.2	15.9
Government	17.9	19.1	21.0
Farm	20.6	21.6	21.6
Total	14.8	15.7	17.9

Source: See text.

ADVANCEMENT OF LABOR PRODUCTIVITY

The gross regional product figures have been used to calculate real product per employee, a measure of the efficiency with which labor is utilized. Theoretically, the most accurate measure of technical efficiency is total factor productivity, calculated as the ratio of output to all factor inputs. [1] However, when calculating total factor productivity, there are problems that result from difficulties in measuring the amount of capital consumed in the productive process. These problems are aggravated by the lack of state or regional data concerning industry capital supplies. Because of such problems, labor productivity figures are often used to approximate changes in technical efficiency. Since labor productivity is a single factor measure, it captures factor substitution, namely substitution of capital for labor, as well as quality improvements in the labor supply. A single factor productivity measure such as real output per employee is a useful and accurate index of efficiency improvements in the utilization of the labor supply, but, because it also reflects factor substitution, one should not use labor productivity change as an indicator of efficiency change for the total economy. [2]

Table 7 contains estimates of the average annual percentage rate of change in real output per employee in the United States, the non-Southeast, and the Southeast. [3] (See appendix table XXVII for estimates of real output per employee.) For the period 1950-70, the overall rate of productivity advance and the industry rates of advance have been very close in the nation and the Southeast. The most rapid rates of increase in labor productivity have occurred in mining, transportation, communication, public utilities, and manufacturing. On the other hand, productivity change has been virtually absent in the construction and service industries.

A decennial view of productivity growth shows that the Southeast's labor productivity grew at an average rate during the 1950s and at a slightly above average rate during the 1960s. (See table 8). During 1960-70, the decennial rate of change for all private nonfarm industries in the Southeast (25.3%) exceeded the average outside the region (18.2%), and the greatest differences occurred in manufacturing and trade. In the Southeast, labor productivity in most industries advanced at a faster rate during the 1960s than during the 1950s; important exceptions to this general rise in productivity during the sixties occurred in the construction and service industries. [4] Outside the Southeast, there was no increase in the rate of productivity change during the 1960s.

TABLE 7

AVERAGE ANNUAL PERCENTAGE RATES OF CHANGE IN REAL PRODUCT PER

EMPLOYEE, UNITED STATES AND SOUTHEAST, 1950-70

Economic Sector	United States	Southeast	Non-Southeast
Private Nonfarm	1.8%	2.0%	1.8%
Mining	4.3	4.6	4.3
Construction	0.1	-0.2	0.2
Manufacturing	2.4	2.5	2.4
Trade	1.4	1.7	1.4
Finance, Insurance and Real Estate	0.9	0.6	1.0
Transportation, Communication and Public Utilities	4.1	4.1	4.1
Services	-0.1	0.1	-0.2

Source: See text.

PER CAPITA OUTPUT PERFORMANCE

A convenient summary indicator of the impact of recent southeastern economic expansion is provided by per capita output figures. Per capita income and per capita output are commonly used measures of the welfare aspects of growth. Table 9 provides a view of trends during 1950-70 in the per capita output achievements of the nation, the non-Southeast, and the Southeast. During this two-decade period, real per capita output advanced at an average annual percentage rate of 2.1% in the nation, 1.8% in the non-Southeast, and 3.1% in the Southeast. During the decade of the 1950s, the decennial rates of increase were as follows: United States 15.8%, non-Southeast 13.6%, and Southeast 26.8%; during the 1960s, the decennial rates of increase were as follows: United States 30.7%, non-Southeast 26.4%, and Southeast 50.7%. The much higher relative per capita output in the Southeast brought about sharp convergence toward the national average per capita output, and, between 1950 and 1970, the Southeast's per capita output increased from 66.1% to 83.5% of the national average. A full discussion of the significance of this trend toward parity with national per capita output standards is provided in chapter IV.

TABLE 8

DECENNIAL RATES OF CHANGE IN REAL PRODUCT PER EMPLOYEE, UNITED STATES

AND SOUTHEAST, 1950-60 AND 1960-70

Economic Sector	United States		Southeast		Non-Southeast	
	1950-60	1960-70	1950-60	1960-70	1950-60	1960-70
Private Nonfarm	18.7%	20.0%	18.0%	25.3%	19.1%	18.2%
Mining	54.9	50.3	56.6	56.7	50.7	51.4
Construction	8.3	-6.2	4.0	-8.5	9.6	-4.3
Manufacturing	21.2	34.0	15.2	43.6	22.6	33.0
Trade	12.3	17.6	12.2	25.9	12.5	16.3
Finance, Insurance and Real Estate	12.4	7.9	2.8	8.3	14.0	8.0
Transportation, Communication and Public Utilities	46.9	53.3	48.2	49.7	47.1	54.2
Services	3.3	-5.3	7.0	-4.6	1.4	-6.3

Source: See text.

TABLE 9

REAL PER CAPITA OUTPUT, UNITED STATES AND

SOUTHEAST, 1950-70

(1958 Dollars)

Year	United States	Southeast	Non-Southeast	Southeast/U.S.
1950	$2340	$1547	$2579	.661
1951	2489	1627	2753	.654
1952	2525	1667	2787	.660
1953	2596	1727	2858	.665
1954	2514	1687	2759	.671
1955	2654	1899	2874	.716
1956	2655	1918	2873	.722
1957	2645	1900	2867	.718
1958	2570	1852	2765	.721
1959	2687	1958	2887	.729
1960	2710	1962	2930	.724
1961	2732	1975	2957	.723
1962	2850	2077	3066	.729
1963	2921	2161	3131	.740
1964	3035	2290	3241	.755
1965	3176	2430	3392	.765
1966	3359	2646	3498	.788
1967	3421	2636	3652	.771
1968	3545	2789	3771	.787
1969	3605	2860	3810	.793
1970	3543	2957	3704	.835

Source: See text.

III. State Developments in Gross State Product during 1950-1970

This chapter provides a survey of economic growth, productivity advance, and structural trends in gross state product during 1950-70 for the individual southeastern states. The analysis points to state variations in growth performance and demonstrates that Florida, Georgia, and North Carolina have been the vanguard in the Southeast's recent economic expansion.

GROWTH TRENDS IN REAL GROSS STATE PRODUCT

Table 10 exhibits the average annual percentage rates of change in real output in the twelve southeastern states for the two-decade period. (The current and constant dollar gross state product figures appear in appendix tables III-XXVI.) Florida's growth performance in aggregate real gross state product (7.0%) ranked well above that of the rest of the southeastern states. Other states achieving growth rates in real gross state product exceeding the regional average (4.6%) were Georgia (5.2%), North Carolina (5.0%), and South Carolina (4.7%). Aggregate growth performance in the remaining states, excluding West Virginia, was very similar, ranging between 4.0% and 4.3%, and it exceeded the national growth rate of 3.6%. West Virginia grew at a very slow rate (1.9%) during the decades after World War II, and low growth characterized all industries in the state.

Economic growth in the southeastern states has been broadly based and has consisted of significant real product increases in most industries. The leading growth states, Florida, Georgia, and North Carolina, matched or exceeded national performance in every industry; Virginia, South Carolina, Kentucky, Mississippi, and Louisiana exceeded national growth in most industries. Especially

TABLE 10

AVERAGE ANNUAL PERCENTAGE RATES OF CHANGE IN REAL PRODUCT, SOUTHEASTERN STATES, 1950-70

Economic Sector	Virginia	West Virginia	North Carolina	South Carolina	Georgia	Florida
Private Nonfarm	4.6%	2.0%	5.4%	5.1%	5.4%	7.4%
Mining	2.9	0.2	4.7	3.8	6.9	5.6
Construction	3.0	2.7	2.4	3.7	2.7	5.1
Manufacturing	4.2	2.5	5.7	5.2	5.2	9.1
Trade	4.8	2.4	4.9	4.7	5.4	7.2
Finance, Insurance and Real Estate	5.3	2.6	6.4	5.8	6.2	7.2
Transportation, Communication and Public Utilities	5.2	2.7	6.6	6.1	6.5	8.5
Services	4.8	2.2	3.9	4.6	5.4	6.3
Government	3.8	2.4	4.4	4.3	4.7	6.2
Farm	0.3	-0.2	1.5	-0.1	1.5	3.8
Total	4.2	1.9	5.0	4.7	5.2	7.0

Economic Sector	Kentucky	Tennessee	Alabama	Mississippi	Arkansas	Louisiana
Private Nonfarm	4.2%	4.6%	4.2%	5.1%	5.0%	4.4%
Mining	1.0	0.9	-0.5	7.6	1.4	6.8
Construction	2.7	1.0	2.2	2.2	0.9	2.8
Manufacturing	5.2	5.4	5.0	7.2	7.4	4.0
Trade	4.1	4.2	3.9	3.4	3.6	4.2
Finance, Insurance and Real Estate	4.9	4.7	4.1	5.4	5.1	4.9
Transportation, Communication and Public Utilities	3.9	4.3	4.5	5.1	4.5	5.1
Services	3.8	3.8	3.7	3.2	3.4	3.2
Government	3.7	3.6	3.9	3.6	3.5	3.8
Farm	1.9	0.7	0.8	1.3	1.7	2.6
Total	4.0	4.2	4.0	4.3	4.3	4.2

Source: See text.

high industry rates of advance were made by North Carolina, Georgia, and Florida in finance, insurance, real estate, transportation, communication, and public utilities. Other notable industry rates of advance were achieved by Florida, Mississippi, and Arkansas in manufacturing and by Florida in trade, services, and government.

Decennial rates of advance in real output are shown in table 11. The most significant increases in real output during the decade 1950-60 were achieved in Florida (110.8%) and Georgia (54.3%). During the 1950s, the majority of southeastern states exceeded the national average decennial rate of growth (37.3%), and only West Virginia (5.4%) was significantly below national performance. During the 1960s, every state except West Virginia (37.7%) exceeded national growth (49.1%), and especially high relative growth was achieved in Florida (84.3%), North Carolina (82.1%), Georgia (76.1%), South

Carolina (75.9%), Tennessee (73.0%), and Arkansas (72.7%). The broad industrial base of economic expansion in the Southeast during the past several decades is evident in the figures in table 11. During the decade 1960-70, Virginia, North Carolina, South

TABLE 11

DECENNIAL RATES OF CHANGE IN REAL PRODUCT, SOUTHEASTERN STATES, 1950-60 AND 1960-70

Economic Sector	Virginia 1950-60	Virginia 1960-70	West Virginia 1950-60	West Virginia 1960-70	North Carolina 1950-60	North Carolina 1960-70	South Carolina 1950-60	South Carolina 1960-70
Private Nonfarm	44.0%	70.0%	5.5%	39.1%	47.0%	93.2%	45.2%	86.1%
Mining	4.9	70.8	-27.4	43.4	47.3	70.1	34.8	56.3
Construction	41.3	29.8	9.0	56.0	16.9	37.7	56.7	31.7
Manufacturing	27.8	78.2	16.2	40.4	42.0	112.5	37.5	98.1
Trade	46.1	74.2	16.3	39.0	42.1	83.8	36.6	84.6
Finance, Insurance and Real Estate	71.0	64.9	41.9	18.1	95.2	76.5	88.8	65.1
Transportation, Communication and Public Utilities	56.6	75.4	21.4	40.0	67.2	113.7	48.1	122.3
Services	59.3	61.8	14.0	35.1	38.1	55.8	48.8	65.1
Government	33.2	58.0	13.4	42.1	47.1	60.9	49.5	56.1
Farm	6.5	0.4	-11.7	-31.1	21.9	9.7	6.1	-8.3
Total	39.7	64.7	5.4	37.7	44.3	82.1	42.4	75.9

Economic Sector	Georgia 1950-60	Georgia 1960-70	Florida 1950-60	Florida 1960-70	Kentucky 1950-60	Kentucky 1960-70	Tennessee 1950-60	Tennessee 1960-70
Private Nonfarm	57.4%	83.2%	119.3%	88.3%	33.6%	71.4%	35.2%	79.5%
Mining	95.8	92.4	128.0	31.8	-17.7	49.3	-17.2	46.2
Construction	31.9	27.8	109.1	27.5	38.1	23.5	4.0	17.2
Manufacturing	46.8	84.8	168.8	100.2	36.7	103.2	33.5	113.9
Trade	49.1	91.3	100.1	98.3	41.6	58.0	39.1	64.2
Finance, Insurance and Real Estate	86.0	77.4	128.9	71.7	71.5	51.5	59.1	58.5
Transportation, Communication and Public Utilities	62.4	118.1	121.5	130.3	28.0	67.8	30.5	78.3
Services	81.3	57.2	98.2	71.0	40.8	50.0	40.2	50.4
Government	54.3	60.0	84.9	80.4	33.8	55.4	31.5	54.4
Farm	21.2	11.1	63.5	28.6	18.4	21.9	5.4	9.9
Total	54.3	76.1	110.8	84.3	32.3	66.0	32.7	73.0

Economic Sector	Alabama 1950-60	Alabama 1960-70	Mississippi 1950-60	Mississippi 1960-70	Arkansas 1950-60	Arkansas 1960-70	Louisiana 1950-60	Louisiana 1960-70
Private Nonfarm	36.6%	66.1%	52.2%	77.1%	38.9%	89.5%	45.9%	62.0%
Mining	-4.8	-0.1	235.2	31.0	8.9	21.1	134.8	57.6
Construction .	50.7	3.2	21.9	27.3	8.1	12.2	34.6	28.8
Manufacturing	28.4	104.6	60.7	147.1	56.2	167.1	15.6	90.2
Trade	38.6	53.4	23.3	56.5	27.2	60.4	45.9	58.2
Finance, Insurance and Real Estate	55.8	43.4	76.6	61.4	60.4	66.5	79.7	43.6
Transportation, Communication and Public Utilities	44.6	67.5	84.2	45.7	37.9	75.6	57.4	71.0
Services	46.0	41.8	38.4	36.6	32.6	47.7	32.2	41.6
Government	62.8	31.0	36.0	49.9	35.4	47.3	42.4	46.8
Farm	14.8	2.5	5.0	23.5	27.2	10.5	18.3	40.1
Total	38.1	57.3	41.4	66.5	36.5	72.7	44.2	59.5

Source: See text.

Carolina, Georgia, Florida and Tennessee exceeded the national decennial rate of advance in every industry except agriculture. Manufacturing was a leading source of economic growth in the Southeast during the 1960s, and decennial rates of advance in excess of 100 % were attained in North Carolina, Florida, Kentucky, Tennessee, Alabama, Mississippi, and Arkansas. Another leading source of growth in the 1960s were the transportation, communication, and public utility industries in which decennial rates of advance exceeding 100 % were achieved in North Carolina, South Carolina, Georgia, and Florida. Farm output increased at a below average rate in all southeastern states except Florida, Kentucky, Mississippi, and Louisiana.

INDUSTRIAL COMPOSITION OF GROSS STATE PRODUCT

Table 12 exhibits the percentage distribution of real gross state product by major industry for 1950, 1960, and 1970. Most states in the Southeast have developed a relatively high commitment to manufacturing compared to national industry concentration patterns. In 1970, the southeastern states with the greatest concentration in

TABLE 12

PERCENTAGE DISTRIBUTION OF REAL PRODUCT, SOUTHEASTERN STATES, 1950, 1960, AND 1970

Economic Sector	Virginia			West Virginia			North Carolina			South Carolina		
	1950	1960	1970	1950	1960	1970	1950	1960	1970	1950	1960	1970
Mining	2.4%	1.8%	1.9%	26.2%	18.1%	18.8%	0.1%	0.1%	0.1%	0.1%	0.1%	0.1%
Construction	4.3	4.3	3.4	3.0	3.1	3.6	4.4	3.6	2.7	3.8	4.2	3.2
Manufacturing	25.4	23.2	25.1	28.0	30.9	31.5	36.2	35.7	41.6	37.5	36.2	40.7
Trade	14.7	15.3	16.2	11.6	12.8	12.9	15.4	15.2	15.3	14.7	14.1	14.8
Finance, Insurance and Real Estate	9.1	11.2	11.2	5.4	7.2	6.2	7.3	9.8	9.5	7.5	9.9	9.3
Transportation, Communication and Public Utilities	9.1	10.2	10.9	9.9	11.5	11.6	6.1	7.1	8.3	5.9	6.1	7.8
Services	8.3	9.5	9.3	6.5	7.1	6.9	8.9	8.5	7.3	8.7	9.0	8.5
Government	21.3	20.3	19.5	6.5	7.0	7.3	10.2	10.4	9.1	13.1	13.7	12.2
Farm	5.5	4.2	2.6	2.8	2.3	1.2	11.0	9.3	5.6	8.5	6.4	3.3

Economic Sector	Georgia			Florida			Kentucky			Tennessee		
	1950	1960	1970	1950	1960	1970	1950	1960	1970	1950	1960	1970
Mining	0.5%	0.7%	0.8%	0.1%	0.1%	0.1%	9.7%	6.0%	5.4%	1.7%	1.0%	0.1%
Construction	4.5	3.9	2.8	6.9	6.8	4.7	4.1	4.3	3.2	5.1	4.0	2.7
Manufacturing	28.4	27.0	28.4	11.6	14.7	17.2	28.7	29.6	36.3	31.7	31.9	39.5
Trade	18.6	18.0	19.5	20.3	19.3	20.7	14.5	15.5	14.7	16.7	17.5	16.6
Finance, Insurance and Real Estate	10.8	13.0	13.1	16.3	17.7	16.5	7.0	9.1	8.3	9.5	11.4	10.5
Transportation, Communication and Public Utilities	9.3	9.8	12.1	9.3	9.8	12.2	9.7	9.4	9.5	8.4	8.3	8.5
Services	8.1	9.5	8.5	14.1	13.2	12.2	7.9	8.4	7.6	9.5	10.0	8.7
Government	12.3	12.2	11.1	14.1	12.4	12.1	9.7	9.9	9.2	10.0	10.0	8.9
Farm	7.5	5.9	3.7	6.6	5.2	3.6	8.7	7.8	5.7	7.3	5.8	3.7

TABLE 12 Cont.

Economic Sector	Alabama 1950	Alabama 1960	Alabama 1970	Mississippi 1950	Mississippi 1960	Mississippi 1970	Arkansas 1950	Arkansas 1960	Arkansas 1970	Louisiana 1950	Louisiana 1960	Louisiana 1970
Mining	3.9%	2.7%	1.7%	1.2%	2.9%	2.3%	2.8%	2.2%	1.6%	6.1%	9.9%	9.7%
Construction	3.9	4.3	2.8	4.5	3.9	3.0	4.9	3.9	2.5	5.3	4.9	4.0
Manufacturing	30.6	28.5	37.0	19.2	22.1	32.3	19.2	21.9	33.9	25.2	20.2	24.1
Trade	16.0	16.0	15.6	18.6	16.6	15.3	18.0	16.9	15.6	16.9	17.1	17.0
Finance, Insurance and Real Estate	9.3	10.5	9.6	7.7	9.8	9.3	8.6	10.1	9.7	9.1	11.4	10.3
Transportation, Communication and Public Utilities	8.3	8.7	9.3	7.5	8.3	8.6	9.6	9.7	9.8	11.1	12.1	13.0
Services	8.9	9.4	8.5	10.2	10.1	8.2	9.6	9.7	8.0	10.6	9.7	8.6
Government	11.7	13.7	11.5	12.5	12.2	10.8	10.4	9.3	8.8	10.7	10.5	9.7
Farm	7.5	6.2	4.1	18.5	14.0	10.2	17.0	15.9	10.1	5.0	4.1	3.6

Source: See text.

manufacturing were North Carolina (41.6%), South Carolina (40.7%), Tennessee (39.5%), and Alabama (37.0%). After World War II, the high manufacturing growth rates in Florida, Mississippi, and Arkansas are clearly documented by sharp increases in the percentage share of gross state product contributed by manufacturing. During 1950-70, manufacturing's share increased from 11.6% to 17.2% in Florida, from 19.2% to 32.3% in Mississippi, and from 19.2% to 33.9% in Arkansas. On the other hand, little or no change occurred in the relative weight of manufacturing in Virginia, Louisiana, and Georgia.

Southeastern states exhibit a rather low concentration on agriculture, and only Mississippi and Arkansas derived a substantial portion of their gross state product from farming. Mining has been relatively unimportant in the Southeast, and only West Virginia, Kentucky, and Louisiana have shown significant activity in this area. Traditionally, the nongovernment service producing industries—trade, finance, insurance, real estate, transportation, communication, public utilities, and services—have been less important to the southeastern states than to the nation as a whole. Some important exceptions to this general rule can be cited in wholesale and retail trade, finance, insurance, and real estate in Florida and Georgia, transportation, communication, and public utilities in Virginia, West Virginia, Florida, Louisiana, and Georgia, and services in Florida. Government activity has been particularly important to the economies of Virginia, South Carolina, Florida, Alabama, Mississippi, and Georgia.

Another manner of viewing relative structural developments during the past several decades is to examine state percentage shares of national industrial output. These figures have been calculated and they appear in table 13. Four states, Florida, North Carolina, Vir-

TABLE 13

SOUTHEASTERN STATES' PERCENTAGE SHARES OF NATIONAL PRODUCT, 1950, 1960, AND 1970

Economic Sector	Virginia 1950	1960	1970	West Virginia 1950	1960	1970	North Carolina 1950	1960	1970	South Carolina 1950	1960	1970
Mining	1.49%	1.22%	1.59%	9.01%	5.34%	5.83%	0.20%	0.25%	0.32%	0.10%	0.12%	0.14%
Construction	1.69	1.78	2.12	0.69	0.56	0.80	1.70	1.49	1.88	0.66	0.77	0.93
Manufacturing	1.54	1.47	1.69	0.98	0.85	0.77	2.13	2.27	3.12	0.99	1.02	1.31
Trade	1.55	1.66	1.88	0.70	0.60	0.54	1.59	1.66	1.97	0.68	0.68	0.81
Finance, Insurance and Real Estate	1.42	1.55	1.72	0.48	0.44	0.35	1.10	1.38	1.63	0.51	0.61	0.68
Transportation, Communication and Public Utilities	1.88	2.02	2.06	1.19	0.99	0.80	1.23	1.41	1.75	0.53	0.54	0.70
Services	1.60	1.81	1.99	0.72	0.59	0.54	1.68	1.64	1.74	0.73	0.77	0.86
Government	3.79	3.67	4.08	0.67	0.55	0.55	1.76	1.89	2.14	1.02	1.11	1.22
Farm	1.72	1.61	1.43	0.50	0.39	0.24	3.36	3.62	3.51	1.17	1.09	0.89
Total	1.80	1.83	2.03	1.03	0.79	0.74	1.70	1.84	2.26	0.78	0.81	0.97

Economic Sector	Georgia 1950	1960	1970	Florida 1950	1960	1970	Kentucky 1950	1960	1970	Tennessee 1950	1960	1970
Mining	0.27%	0.43%	0.46%	0.43%	0.81%	0.81%	4.12%	2.77%	3.15%	0.80%	0.54%	0.61%
Construction	1.46	1.44	1.69	2.27	3.54	4.15	1.16	1.20	1.36	1.62	1.26	1.36
Manufacturing	1.41	1.55	1.85	0.58	1.18	1.63	1.24	1.27	1.67	1.54	1.54	2.13
Trade	1.61	1.76	2.19	1.79	2.63	3.39	1.09	1.14	1.17	1.42	1.45	1.54
Finance, Insurance and Real Estate	1.38	1.64	1.95	2.12	3.10	3.57	0.79	0.86	0.87	1.19	1.21	1.29
Transportation, Communication and Public Utilities	1.57	1.76	2.22	1.61	2.45	3.28	1.44	1.27	1.23	1.40	1.25	1.29
Services	1.22	1.56	1.65	2.26	3.18	3.70	1.09	1.09	1.11	1.47	1.46	1.49
Government	1.78	2.01	2.26	2.09	2.82	3.58	1.24	1.21	1.32	1.43	1.38	1.49
Farm	1.91	2.05	2.01	1.74	2.51	2.86	1.94	2.03	2.19	1.82	1.70	1.65
Total	1.47	1.66	1.96	1.50	2.30	2.87	1.29	1.24	1.39	1.44	1.39	1.63

Economic Sector	Alabama 1950	1960	1970	Mississippi 1950	1960	1970	Arkansas 1950	1960	1970	Louisiana 1950	1960	1970
Mining	1.51%	1.17%	0.89%	0.25%	0.68%	0.67%	0.56%	0.49%	0.46%	2.64%	5.06%	6.07%
Construction	1.00	1.12	1.07	0.60	0.54	0.64	0.64	0.52	0.53	1.53	1.53	1.82
Manufacturing	1.21	1.16	1.54	0.39	0.63	0.76	0.39	0.45	0.78	1.12	0.97	1.19
Trade	1.10	1.12	1.12	0.67	0.60	0.61	0.63	0.59	0.62	1.31	1.40	1.43
Finance, Insurance and Real Estate	0.95	0.95	0.91	0.41	0.46	0.50	0.44	0.45	0.51	1.04	1.19	1.15
Transportation, Communication and Public Utilities	1.13	1.12	1.09	0.53	0.55	0.56	0.66	0.62	0.63	1.68	1.81	1.80
Services	1.12	1.16	1.12	0.67	0.65	0.61	0.62	0.58	0.58	1.50	1.40	1.35
Government	1.36	1.61	1.49	0.75	0.75	0.79	0.61	0.61	0.63	1.39	1.44	1.49
Farm	1.53	1.55	1.41	1.97	1.83	2.00	1.77	1.99	1.95	1.14	1.19	1.48
Total	1.17	1.18	1.26	0.61	0.62	0.70	0.60	0.59	0.69	1.31	1.39	1.49

Source: See text.

ginia, and Georgia, contributed 2% or more to the nation's gross national product. Florida contributed shares exceeding 3% of national output in all industries except mining, manufacturing, and agriculture. Other notable industry contributions were: North Carolina in farm and manufacturing, Virginia in government, and West Virginia, Louisiana, and Kentucky in mining. In all other cases, state shares of national industry output were less than 3%. West Virginia, Mississippi, and Arkansas made the smallest impact on national production and contributed less than 1% to gross national product; industry shares exceeded 1% in mining in West Virginia and in agriculture in Mississippi and Arkansas.

LABOR PRODUCTIVITY CHANGE DURING 1950-70

Table 14 exhibits average annual percentage rates of change in real product per employee. The national rate of increase (1.8%) for all

TABLE 14

AVERAGE ANNUAL PERCENTAGE RATES OF CHANGE IN REAL PRODUCT PER EMPLOYEE, SOUTHEASTERN

STATES, 1950-70

Economic Sector	Virginia	West Virginia	North Carolina	South Carolina	Georgia	Florida
Private Nonfarm	1.6%	2.4%	2.1%	2.2%	2.3%	1.6%
Mining	4.9	4.8	4.0	2.0	4.2	4.0
Construction	-0.1	0.7	-1.1	-0.2	-0.6	0.2
Manufacturing	1.8	2.7	2.8	2.7	2.7	3.0
Trade	1.7	2.0	1.5	1.9	2.0	1.8
Finance, Insurance, and Real Estate	0.7	0.3	0.7	0.3	0.9	0.2
Transportation, Communication and Public Utilities	4.1	4.0	3.9	4.3	4.2	4.0
Services	0.0	0.1	0.0	0.8	1.4	-0.5

Economic Sector	Kentucky	Tennessee	Alabama	Mississippi	Arkansas	Louisiana
Private Nonfarm	2.0%	1.8%	2.0%	2.1%	2.1%	2.1%
Mining	4.9	4.0	5.2	2.8	3.4	3.6
Construction	-0.1	-0.6	-0.6	-1.1	0.8	0.5
Manufacturing	2.2	2.2	2.8	3.2	3.2	3.0
Trade	1.6	1.8	1.5	1.4	1.6	1.8
Finance, Insurance and Real Estate	0.9	0.5	0.3	0.7	0.2	0.7
Transportation, Communication and Public Utilities	4.0	3.8	4.0	4.2	4.1	4.2
Services	-0.3	0.3	-0.1	0.3	-0.1	-0.7

Source: See text.

private nonfarm industries was surpassed by every southeastern state except Virginia (1.6%), Florida (1.6%), and Tennessee (1.8%); in the remaining southeastern states, productivity growth varied between 2.0% and 2.4%. Despite the slightly more rapid rate of productivity advance in most southeastern states for the aggregate private nonfarm sector, individual industry differences in productivity growth between the nation and the southeastern states were generally minor. The construction industry experienced a negative movement in productivity during the two-decade period, and the service industry showed little or no significant increase in productivity. On the other hand, mining and transportation, communication, and public utilities showed high rates of productivity change, generally in excess of 4%.

Decennial rates of productivity change during the 1950s and 1960s are shown in table 15. The calculations for the 1950s show that only in West Virginia, Georgia, Mississippi, and Louisiana did rates of productivity change for the total private nonfarm sector exceed national performance. However, during the 1960s, every state except Florida surpassed national productivity growth. The relatively high rate of labor-productivity advance consisted of a variety of industry contributions, and it is difficult to generalize across states. For example, in North and South Carolina, Mississippi, Alabama, Arkansas, and Louisiana, the greatest relative productivity advance occurred in manufacturing; in Georgia, the greatest relative advance occurred in trade; and, in Virginia and Kentucky, the greatest relative advance occurred in mining. In spite of these variations, the industrial pattern of productivity growth was quite similar in the southeastern states and the nation.

TABLE 15

DECENNIAL RATES OF CHANGE IN REAL PRODUCT PER EMPLOYEE, SOUTHEASTERN STATES, 1950-60 AND 1960-70

Economic Sector	Virginia 1950-60	Virginia 1960-70	West Virginia 1950-60	West Virginia 1960-70	North Carolina 1950-60	North Carolina 1960-70	South Carolina 1950-60	South Carolina 1960-70
Private Nonfarm	15.5%	20.7%	24.7%	29.8%	16.4%	31.2%	18.6%	30.8%
Mining	38.7	87.6	58.4	61.8	51.7	43.9	1.1	47.1
Construction	6.8	-8.7	15.5	0.4	-13.9	-6.9	9.7	-11.5
Manufacturing	6.6	34.2	22.6	38.3	16.6	50.7	15.6	45.9
Trade	12.5	24.7	14.4	28.0	9.1	24.5	8.5	34.2
Finance, Insurance and Real Estate	9.7	5.5	7.8	0.1	7.6	6.9	-9.6	18.4
Transportation, Communication and Public Utilities	49.5	50.0	46.8	49.8	42.6	49.7	53.9	51.1
Services	10.2	-9.0	-1.2	3.4	8.1	-7.3	14.5	2.0

TABLE 15 Cont.

Economic Sector	Georgia 1950-60	Georgia 1960-70	Florida 1950-60	Florida 1960-70	Kentucky 1950-60	Kentucky 1960-70	Tennessee 1950-60	Tennessee 1960-70
Private Nonfarm	24.8%	27.0%	16.7%	18.1%	16.4%	26.2%	12.5%	27.0%
Mining	46.9	56.1	66.3	30.2	42.8	81.3	41.8	52.5
Construction	-3.9	-7.6	14.7	-9.6	6.1	-6.9	2.7	-13.0
Manufacturing	23.4	36.3	33.0	38.0	11.6	38.5	5.7	45.3
Trade	14.2	30.1	13.2	26.9	11.7	22.7	16.1	23.2
Finance, Insurance and Real Estate	44.9	14.5	-11.5	7.3	11.8	6.4	0.2	9.9
Transportation, Communication and Public Utilities	50.4	49.6	46.2	49.3	44.8	49.3	40.2	49.2
Services	35.7	-2.6	-2.9	-6.6	1.1	-6.5	8.5	-2.2

Economic Sector	Alabama 1950-60	Alabama 1960-70	Mississippi 1950-60	Mississippi 1960-70	Arkansas 1950-60	Arkansas 1960-70	Louisiana 1950-60	Louisiana 1960-70
Private Nonfarm	15.6%	27.9%	18.9%	25.6%	15.2%	30.6%	20.9%	26.0%
Mining	76.4	56.4	30.1	35.0	30.7	48.1	48.6	37.0
Construction	-1.6	-9.3	-8.4	-11.9	-3.1	-11.7	15.2	-4.2
Manufacturing	17.1	49.8	15.8	63.0	15.5	62.8	18.0	54.0
Trade	10.7	21.3	7.1	24.3	11.4	22.7	13.4	25.5
Finance, Insurance and Real Estate	-5.1	12.3	9.9	3.3	0.6	4.2	9.6	3.5
Transportation, Communication and Public Utilities	46.3	50.9	85.6	23.8	47.2	52.2	46.3	54.5
Services	0.7	-3.1	6.6	-11.8	4.5	-6.2	-5.4	-7.8

Source: See text.

TABLE 16

REAL PER CAPITA OUTPUT, SOUTHEASTERN STATES, 1950-70
(1958 Dollars)

Year	Virginia	West Virginia	North Carolina	South Carolina	Georgia	Florida
1950	$1922	$1832	$1530	$1316	$1515	$1925
1951	2030	1977	1571	1410	1664	1914
1952	2052	1960	1593	1487	1693	1945
1953	2058	1971	1668	1547	1765	2015
1954	2082	1794	1645	1408	1705	2001
1955	2215	1972	1792	1601	1941	2183
1956	2225	2116	1790	1597	1981	2242
1957	2174	2173	1733	1542	1936	2226
1958	2119	1988	1779	1470	1899	2150
1959	2210	2090	1895	1594	2012	2258
1960	2236	2094	1968	1665	2040	2270
1961	2254	2102	2006	1675	2230	2190
1962	2371	2305	2125	1809	2160	2268
1963	2407	2451	2170	1865	2290	2337
1964	2531	2457	2316	2016	2439	2467
1965	2650	2638	2451	2192	2602	2576
1966	2751	2803	2642	2322	2764	2685
1967	2825	2859	2709	2331	2823	2795
1968	2970	2881	2919	2496	2966	2932
1969	3043	2881	3010	2556	3061	3103
1970	3157	3056	3211	2695	3091	3051

TABLE 16 Cont.

Year	Kentucky	Tennessee	Alabama	Mississippi	Arkansas	Louisiana
1950	$1551	$1556	$1363	$ 992	$1112	$1738
1951	1675	1571	1470	1020	1184	1799
1952	1790	1588	1481	1081	1245	1795
1953	1833	1715	1546	1165	1300	1876
1954	1761	1683	1503	1171	1325	1856
1955	1958	1802	1687	1333	1503	2008
1956	2016	1829	1710	1281	1507	2053
1957	2012	1818	1700	1250	1478	2113
1958	1923	1771	1651	1262	1456	1996
1959	2027	1891	1748	1386	1633	2066
1960	1988	1905	1764	1381	1624	2065
1961	2009	1981	1732	1441	1733	2090
1962	2149	2097	1795	1491	1822	2148
1963	2287	2137	1882	1602	1884	2231
1964	2350	2254	2025	1700	2036	2375
1965	2529	2435	2153	1817	2116	2512
1966	2716	2602	2280	1918	2262	2686
1967	2737	2648	2319	2010	2293	2768
1968	2928	2826	2461	2151	2465	2919
1969	3009	2879	2556	2154	2562	2918
1970	3114	2997	2632	2295	2603	2946

Source: See text.

PER CAPITA GROSS STATE PRODUCT

Per capita levels of real gross state product are shown in table 16, and it is clear that great progress in per capita performance was made during the past two decades in each southeastern state. Every state exceeded the national growth rate in per capita output (2.1%), and the leading states were Mississippi, Arkansas, Georgia, North Carolina, South Carolina, and Kentucky. (See table 17.) Decennial rates of increase in real per capita gross state product appear in table 18, and they provide evidence of a sharp relative growth spurt in the Southeast during the decade of the 1960s. During the period 1950-60, the majority of southeastern states exceeded the nation's decennial rate of increase in real per capita output (15.8%), but the performance of Virginia, West Virginia, Florida, and Louisiana was similar to national growth. During the period 1960-70, every southeastern state surpassed national per capita growth performance. In both decades, North and South Carolina, Kentucky, Mississippi, and Arkansas approximately doubled the nation's rate of increase in per capita output, and Georgia and Alabama also advanced at a rate significantly faster than the national average.

TABLE 17

AVERAGE ANNUAL PERCENTAGE RATES OF CHANGE IN REAL PER CAPITA OUTPUT,

SOUTHEASTERN STATES, 1950-70

State	Rate of Change
Virginia	2.4%
West Virginia	2.4
North Carolina	3.6
South Carolina	3.4
Georgia	3.6
Florida	2.2
Kentucky	3.4
Tennessee	3.1
Alabama	3.1
Mississippi	4.1
Arkansas	4.1
Louisiana	2.5

Source: See text.

TABLE 18

DECENNIAL RATES OF CHANGE IN REAL PER CAPITA OUTPUT, SOUTHEASTERN

STATES, 1950-60 AND 1960-70

State	1950-60	1960-70
Virginia	16.3%	41.2%
West Virginia	14.3	45.9
North Carolina	28.6	63.2
South Carolina	26.5	61.9
Georgia	34.7	51.5
Florida	17.9	34.4
Kentucky	28.2	56.6
Tennessee	22.4	57.3
Alabama	29.4	49.2
Mississippi	39.2	66.2
Arkansas	46.0	60.3
Louisiana	18.8	42.7

Source: See text.

The much more rapid per capita output growth in the southeastern states compared to the nation as a whole is clearly depicted by the relative per capita output figures in table 19.

TABLE 19

PER CAPITA OUTPUT RELATIVES, SOUTHEASTERN STATES/UNITED STATES,

1950, 1960, AND 1970

State	1950	1960	1970
Virginia	.822	.825	.891
West Virginia	.783	.773	.863
North Carolina	.654	.726	.906
South Carolina	.562	.614	.761
Georgia	.648	.753	.872
Florida	.823	.838	.861
Kentucky	.663	.734	.879
Tennessee	.665	.703	.846
Alabama	.583	.651	.743
Mississippi	.424	.510	.648
Arkansas	.475	.600	.735
Louisiana	.743	.762	.831

Source: See text.

During 1950-70, significant gains toward parity with national standards of per capita output were made by North Carolina (65.4% to 90.6%), Kentucky (66.3% to 87.9%), Tennessee (66.5% to 84.6%), Georgia (64.8% to 87.2%), South Carolina (56.2% to 76.1%), Arkansas (47.5% to 73.5%), Mississippi (42.4% to 64.8%), and Alabama (58.3% to 74.3%). A further discussion of the consequences of this convergence toward national per capita output standards is provided in chapter IV.

Table 20 exhibits relative per capita output developments within the Southeast during the past two decades, and the figures clearly point to convergence within the region.

Those states which had achieved relatively high per capita output levels at the beginning of the period, Virginia, West Virginia, Florida, and Louisiana, declined steadily toward the average per capita standard for the region as a whole. On the contrary, two states that had lagged far behind the average performance of the region, Mississippi and Arkansas, moved closer toward parity with regional standards of per capita output. At the same time, North Carolina, Georgia, and Kentucky advanced as leaders in the region's per capita output performance. Further analysis of convergence of per capita output levels within the Southeast is provided in chapter IV.

TABLE 20

PER CAPITA OUTPUT RELATIVES, SOUTHEASTERN STATES/SOUTHEAST,

1950, 1960, AND 1970

State	1950	1960	1970
Virginia	1.242	1.140	1.068
West Virginia	1.184	1.067	1.034
North Carolina	.989	1.003	1.086
South Carolina	.851	.849	.911
Georgia	.979	1.040	1.045
Florida	1.244	1.157	1.032
Kentucky	1.003	1.013	1.053
Tennessee	1.006	.971	1.014
Alabama	.881	.899	.890
Mississippi	.641	.704	.776
Arkansas	.719	.828	.880
Louisiana	1.124	1.053	.996

Source: See text.

IV. Convergence-Divergence in Per Capita Output Trends

Variation in recent per capita growth performance among the southeastern region, the individual southeastern states, and the United States is examined in this chapter. The analysis focuses on whether recent growth performance in the Southeast will lead to future parity with national per capita output levels. Regression analysis is used to determine the degree of change in per capita output over time, and measures of both absolute and relative per capita output differences are used to judge the significance of southeastern convergence with national per capita output standards.

CONVERGENCE TO NATIONAL PER CAPITA OUTPUT LEVELS

During the period 1950-70, per capita output in the Southeast grew at an annual percentage rate of 3.1% compared to 2.1% in the United States, and continuation of this growth disparity would suggest that per capita output levels in the Southeast will converge on the national standard. However, an exchange of views on regional trends in per capita income levels suggests that one's willingness to accept the thesis of steady regional convergence toward parity with national per capita standards depends on the measure chosen to depict regional variation from national performance. [1] If one utilizes a relative measure of per capita income levels, one can easily point to a steady trend toward convergence in the past decades. [2] However, E. J. R. Booth pointed out that measures of the absolute dollar difference between southern and national per capita income levels lead one to conclude that there is no trend toward convergence. For the period 1948-60, Booth demonstrated that linear trends in absolute per capita income differences between the South and the rest of the United States point to a widening gap with the South falling further and further behind. [3] Booth suggests that both an absolute and a relative test should be used to determine whether per capita income trends demonstrate convergence or divergence.

In this chapter, I have utilized the per capita output series de-veloped in this study to analyze the issue of southeastern convergence toward national per capita output standards. For the Southeast, I have constructed a relative measure of per capita output differences, per capita output in the Southeast/per capita output in the nation, and an absolute measure of real (1958 dollars) differences, per capita output in the Southeast minus per capita output in the nation. Simi-larly, relative and absolute measures of per capita output differences were constructed for each southeastern state. For each of these measures, the trend over time, 1950-70, was estimated by a linear and a logarithmic regression equation. [4] In each case the null hypoth-esis that the regression coefficient (b) was equal to zero was tested in Student's t distribution against the alternative hypothesis that (b) was not equal to zero. Since per capita output in all southeastern states was below the national average, rejection of the null hypothesis would give evidence of significant convergence (b > 0) or significant divergence (b < 0). The results from the regression analysis are summarized in tables 21 and 22.

The relative measure of per capita output differences suggests that the Southeast and each southeastern state achieved a significant narrowing in its relative backwardness compared to national per capita levels. (See table 21.) The logarithmic trends generally provide a better fit than the linear trends, but the differences are minor, and one can argue from either approach that a significant relative ad-vance in per capita output levels was made by the southeastern region and states during the past two decades.

Trends in the measure of real absolute per capita output dif-ferences indicate that the southeastern region as a whole and North Carolina, Georgia, Kentucky, Tennessee, and Arkansas achieved a significant narrowing of their absolute per capita output gap with the national standard. (See table 22.) On the basis of the results in tables 21 and 22, it is clear that the Southeast as a whole and these five states satisfy both the absolute and relative test of convergence toward parity with national per capita output levels. In Virginia, a signifi-cant negative trend in real absolute per capita output differences was found, and this suggests that Virginia has diverged from parity with national per capita output levels. In all other states, the trends in absolute differences were not strong enough to accept either the notion of convergence or divergence.

However, the results in tables 21 and 22 do not necessarily mean

TABLE 21

LINEAR AND LOGARITHMIC TRENDS IN RELATIVE PER CAPITA OUTPUT LEVELS, 1950-70

(United States = 100)

Area	Linear Trends			Logarithmic Trends		
	Intercept (a)	Slope[a] (b)	Coefficient of Determination (r^2)	Intercept (a)	Slope[a] (b)	Coefficient of Determination (r^2)
Southeast	65.3	.7668***	.9248	1.8166	.00457***	.9271
Virginia	81.2	.1714**	.3556	1.9095	.00089***	.3588
West Virginia	75.7	.3909***	.4603	1.8792	.00213***	.4527
North Carolina	60.9	1.1656***	.9237	1.7898	.00689***	.9403
South Carolina	54.5	.8527***	.8562	1.7398	.00578***	.8654
Georgia	65.5	1.0297*	.9610	1.8186	.00593*	.9585
Florida	79.6	.1999**	.2089	1.9010	.00107***	.2107
Kentucky	67.7	.8142***	.8782	1.8326	.00465***	.8811
Tennessee	62.8	.9082***	.9398	1.8009	.00545***	.9461
Alabama	58.4	.6288***	.8671	1.7676	.00421***	.8725
Mississippi	41.6	1.0294***	.9600	1.6250	.00867***	.9586
Arkansas	47.7	1.2636***	.9743	1.6846	.00926***	.9632
Louisiana	72.5	.4648	.7517	1.8608	.00262	.7499

[a]The significance of the regression coefficients is shown by an * where * = P ≤ .05, ** = P ≤ .01, and *** = P ≤ .001.

Source: See text.

TABLE 22

LINEAR AND LOGARITHMIC TRENDS IN REAL ABSOLUTE PER CAPITA OUTPUT

DIFFERENCES, 1950-70

(State or Region - United States)

Area	Linear Trends			Logarithmic Trends		
	Intercept (a)	Slope[a] (b)	Coefficient of Determination (r^2)	Intercept (a)	Slope[a] (b)	Coefficient of Determination (r^2)
Southeast	-827.7	6.55**	.4403	-2.9186	.00379**	.4246
Virginia	-440.6	-4.94*	.2632	-2.6461	-.00411*	.2379
West Virginia	-573.7	-0.59***	.0024	-2.7558	-.00039***	.0019
North Carolina	-952.7	18.84	.7166	-2.9954	.01211	.5952
South Carolina	-1083.8	3.72***	.1781	-3.0341	.00157***	.1761
Georgia	-829.7	16.33	.8213	-2.9248	.01070	.7968
Florida	-475.6	-5.01***	.1470	-2.6736	-.00420***	.1457
Kentucky	-775.4	9.88***	.5641	-2.8938	.00668***	.5180
Tennessee	-894.4	10.46	.6464	-2.9549	.00597	.6066
Alabama	-981.3	-2.41	.0696	-2.9917	-.00099	.0628
Mississippi	-1381.1	1.58***	.0266	-3.1400	.00051***	.0280
Arkansas	-1248.6	13.29	.6632	-3.0968	.00510	.6591
Louisiana	-651.1	0.28	.0012	-2.8116	.00010	.0003

[a]See note a to Table 21.

Source: See text.

that the majority of southeastern states will not achieve parity with the nation in the near future. Because of differences in the size of the per capita output base, temporary or short-run maintenance of the absolute dollar gap between a state and the nation can occur while the state is making steady progress toward parity with national per capita output standards. In order to assert the notion of convergence toward parity with national per capita output levels, the rate of increase in per capita output in states with below average per capita output levels must significantly exceed the rate of increase for the nation as a whole. [5] Linear and logarithmic trends in real per capita output during 1950-70 were calculated for the United States, the Southeast, and the individual southeastern states. (See table 23.) Examination of the linear trends indicates that in all cases except Virginia, West Virginia, Florida, and Alabama, the coefficient of per capita output advance in the southeastern states exceeded the national average. The logarithmic trends in real per capita output growth shown in table 23 provide a better fit to the per capita output data than the linear trends, and the trend rate of increase in every state exceeded the national average; however, in Virginia and Florida the differences were minor.

TABLE 23

LINEAR AND LOGARITHMIC TRENDS IN REAL PER CAPITA OUTPUT, 1950-70

Area	Linear Trends			Logarithmic Trends		
	Intercept (a)	Slope[a] (b)	Coefficient of Determination (r^2)	Intercept (a)	Slope[a] (b)	Coefficient of Determination (r^2)
Southeast	1450.9	67.12	.9207	3.1837	.01348	.9487
United States	2278.6	60.57	.8914	3.3670	.00892	.9102
Virginia	1838.0	55.64	.8897	3.2764	.00982	.9151
West Virginia	1704.9	59.98	.8775	3.2463	.01105	.8893
North Carolina	1326.0	79.42	.9134	3.1568	.01581	.9535
South Carolina	1194.9	64.30	.8792	3.1068	.01471	.9069
Georgia	1448.9	76.90	.9419	3.1869	.01492	.9642
Florida	1803.0	55.57	.8866	3.2680	.01000	.9135
Kentucky	1503.2	70.45	.9052	3.1996	.01358	.9324
Tennessee	1384.2	71.03	.9177	3.1672	.01449	.9488
Alabama	1297.3	58.16	.9084	3.1344	.01315	.9381
Mississippi	897.6	62.15	.9378	2.9919	.01759	.9678
Arkansas	1030.1	73.87	.9630	3.0515	.01819	.9835
Louisiana	1627.6	60.85	.8996	3.2277	.01155	.9264

[a]All coefficients of the trend in per capita output were significant at $P \leq .001$.

Source: See text.

Of course, one's willingness to accept the argument for convergence depends on one's view of the representativeness of the period 1950-70 as a basis for extrapolating future per capita output levels. Assuming that the period is representative of the future, extrapolating on the basis of logarithmic trends in per capita output suggests that it will be approximately forty years before the Southeast achieves parity with national per capita production levels. [6] Within the Southeast, North Carolina, Georgia, Kentucky, Tennessee, and Arkansas have achieved very high per capita output growth during the past two decades, and continuation of this relatively high growth will result in future convergence with national per capita output levels. However, the optimistic assumption of continued relative prosperity for these states indicates that it will still be three or four decades before they reach national per capita production standards. In most of the remaining southeastern states, a case can be made for convergence, but it appears that this phenomenon is in the distant future. In Florida and Virginia, recent per capita output trends compared with national performance have resulted in a widening of real differences, and it is difficult to make a case for convergence for these states.

CONVERGENCE WITHIN THE SOUTHEAST

The data on absolute per capita output levels and per capita growth trends in the southeastern states surveyed in chapter III provide some insight into movements of convergence and divergence within the Southeast during the past two decades. This section uses the techniques developed earlier in this chapter to formally analyze the significance of trends in relative and absolute state per capita output differences.

The overall picture revealed by linear and logarithmic trends in relative and absolute per capita output differences within the Southeast during the past two decades is one of strong convergence. (See tables 24 and 25.) Four states, Virginia, West Virginia, Florida, and Louisiana, began the period with per capita output levels well above the regional average. During the two-decade period, each state suffered a significant relative decline, and, by 1970, each was close to parity with the regional average. (See tables 20 and 24.) Of the states that began the period with per capita output below the regional standard, only Alabama failed to achieve a significant relative advance.

Significant downward convergence to regional per capita output standards was shown in the absolute real per capita output measure by Virginia, West Virginia, Florida, and Louisiana. (See table 25.) On the other hand, significant upward convergence to regional per capita output was shown by North Carolina, Tennessee, and Arkansas. Georgia and Kentucky began the period close to the regional average and made absolute gains during 1950-70; South Carolina, Alabama, and Mississippi began the period far below the regional average and fell further behind during 1950-70. [7]

This chapter has used several alternative measures of trends in per

TABLE 24

LINEAR AND LOGARITHMIC TRENDS IN RELATIVE PER CAPITA OUTPUT LEVELS WITHIN

THE SOUTHEAST, 1950-70

(Southeast = 100)

Area	Linear Trends			Logarithmic Trends		
	Intercept (a)	Slope[a] (b)	Coefficient of Determination (r^2)	Intercept (a)	Slope[a] (b)	Coefficient of Determination (r^2)
Virginia	123.6	-.9604***	.9044	3.0926	-.00365***	.9075
West Virginia	115.5	-.6194***	.4945	3.0624	-.00243***	.4938
North Carolina	93.9	.5370*	.6183	2.9732	.00233*	.6097
South Carolina	83.8	.2422***	.2133	2.9233	.00122***	.2084
Georgia	100.7	.3430***	.4703	3.0016	.00155***	.4842
Florida	121.2	-.8981	.8441	3.0843	-.00348	.8418
Kentucky	103.8	.0216**	.0059	3.0159	.00010**	.0067
Tennessee	96.5	.2012	.3036	2.9843	.00089	.3031
Alabama	89.3	-.0666***	.1463	2.9507	-.00033***	.1456
Mississippi	64.2	.6666***	.8761	2.8083	.00411***	.8701
Arkansas	73.6	.8795***	.8716	2.8679	.00470***	.8690
Louisiana	110.6	-.4712	.7554	3.0440	-.00193	.7576

[a]See note a to Table 21.

Source: See text.

TABLE 25

LINEAR AND LOGARITHMIC TRENDS IN REAL ABSOLUTE PER CAPITA OUTPUT DIFFERENCES

WITHIN THE SOUTHEAST, 1950-70

(State - Southeast)

Area	Linear Trends			Logarithmic Trends		
	Intercept (a)	Slope[a] (b)	Coefficient of Determination (r^2)	Intercept (a)	Slope[a] (b)	Coefficient of Determination (r^2)
Virginia	387.1	-11.48*	.8205	2.6076	-.01924*	.7228
West Virginia	254.0	-7.14***	.2631	2.4103	-.02130***	.2295
North Carolina	-125.0	12.30	.6037	-2.5407	.24138	.7139
South Carolina	-256.1	-2.83***	.1059	-2.3919	-.00539**	.1440
Georgia	-2.0	9.78***	.6747	.8693	.08667***	.4391
Florida	352.1	-11.55*	.6596	2.5907	-.02607*	.4977
Kentucky	52.3	3.33*	.2559	1.5801	.02679*	.2252
Tennessee	-66.7	3.91***	.2968	-1.8167	.12459***	.2890
Alabama	-153.6	-8.96**	.8454	-2.2136	-.01599**	.8726
Mississippi	-553.4	-4.97**	.3338	-2.7439	-.00349**	.3313
Arkansas	-420.9	6.74***	.4275	-2.6226	.00815*	.3753
Louisiana	176.6	-6.27	.5447	2.4837	-.05844*	.2705

[a]See note a to Table 21.

Source: See text.

capita output differences, in conjunction with trends in real per capita output, to evaluate the significance of southeastern convergence toward parity with national per capita output levels and convergence within the Southeast. The results indicate that despite the recent marked progress of the Southeast toward parity with national per capita production, the region still faces a considerable period of relative backwardness. The growth process is complicated and long-run changes such as compensating for decades of stagnation and slow growth require time and do not take place overnight. However, the future for the Southeast appears to be very bright and there are strong grounds for optimism. Recent per capita growth trends within the Southeast have indicated a greater degree of balance among states with several new growth leaders, North Carolina, Georgia, and Kentucky, joining the previous leaders, Virginia and Florida.

V. The Role of Productivity in the Southeast's Economic Growth

American economic growth has become increasingly dependent on qualitative improvements in the use of resources. These qualitative or efficiency improvements in resource utilization are generally referred to as changes in productivity, and they reflect advancement in technology, advances and extensions of knowledge through increased education, economies of scale, organizational improvements, and other related factors.

Edward Denison suggested that qualitative factors such as increases in education, advances in knowledge, and economies of scale were responsible for 52% of aggregate growth in the American economy during 1929-57. [1] John W. Kendrick argued that during 1889-1953 productivity change accounted for approximately half of the increase in real output and three-fourths of the increase in real output per capita. [2] In examining the sources of labor productivity increase during this period, Kendrick noted that in the majority of industries substitution of capital for labor had occurred at an average annual rate of 0.1-0.3%; from this he concluded that factor substitution had not been a major factor in labor saving. [3] Robert Solow examined the sources of increase in labor productivity for the period 1909-49 and asserted that almost 90% of the advance was due to technical or efficiency improvements in the utilization of labor, and the small residual was due to factor substitution. [4] F. C. Mills argued that increases in labor productivity were responsible for significant gains in consumer welfare during the late nineteenth and twentieth centuries. [5] Theodore W. Schultz hypothesized that increased investment in education may have been responsible for 35% of American economic growth during recent decades. [6] Each of these studies concluded that a large portion of recent American economic growth has resulted from qualitative improvements or intangible factors such as productivity increase, technological change, educational advance, organizational improvement, and related factors. As the fundamental economic problem of scarcity has been handled with increased efficiency, quantitative increases in the amount of capital and labor consumed in the productive process have accounted for a diminishing portion of our growth.

THE CONCEPT OF THE PRODUCTIVITY INCREMENT

Using a statistical technique developed by F. C. Mills, it is possible to separate the portion of increased output that was due to improved efficiency in the utilization of labor from the portion that was due to simple aggregative increases in the supply of labor. [7] The procedure attempts to estimate output in the terminal year (t) in the absence of efficiency change between the base year (o) and year (t). The technique works as follows:

$$(Q/L)_o \cdot (L)_t \ = \ Q_t^*$$

where Q = real output, L = the total number of employees, o and t are as defined above, and Q_t^* = the estimate of real output in the absence of labor productivity change. The difference between Q_t and Q_t^* equals the change in output due to the advance of labor productivity between year (o) and year (t); in Mills's terminology, this is the productivity increment. Since this study uses a single-factor productivity measure, real output per employee, increases in real output not attributed to increases in the labor supply are attributed to improvements in the utilization of labor. [8] The procedure captures any factor that results in an increase in the average output per employee; this can be a pure productivity change such as increased efficiency in the organization of labor or it may simply be a substitution of capital for labor in the production function. It should be made clear that the productivity increment as calculated in this study is a rather broad residual measure of the impact of efficiency change on increased output, and it includes any increase in output that cannot be attributed directly to quantitative increases in the labor supply. The percentage change in real output contributed by productivity advance can be calculated as follows:

$$\frac{Q_t \ - \ Q_t^*}{Q_t \ - \ Q_o} \ = \ q^p$$

Similarly, the percentage change in real output contributed by quantitative increases in the labor supply can be taken as the residual percentage share as follows:

$$\frac{Q_t^* - Q_o}{Q_t - Q_o} = q^1$$

THE CONTRIBUTION OF LABOR PRODUCTIVITY CHANGE TO
AGGREGATE AND PER CAPITA OUTPUT

The estimated percentage shares of industry output that resulted from improvements in labor productivity are shown in tables 26 and 27. It is clear from the figures that productivity advance has accounted for a substantial portion of the increase in real output during the past two decades. For the total private nonfarm sector, only in Virginia (48.0%) and Florida (36.2%) was the calculated percentage share of output due to productivity advance less than 50%. The differences among the United States, Southeast, and individual southeastern states were slight in most all cases; the only major exception

TABLE 26

PERCENTAGE INCREASE IN REAL PRODUCT DURING 1950-70 DUE TO

PRODUCTIVITY ADVANCE, UNITED STATES AND

SOUTHEAST

Economic Sector	United States	Southeast
Private Nonfarm	56.6%	52.4%
Mining	100.0[a]	100.0
Construction	5.4	0.0
Manufacturing	74.5	61.4
Trade	46.4	47.9
Finance, Insurance and Real Estate	30.8	15.3
Transportation, Communication and Public Utilities	92.3	83.1
Services	0.0[b]	3.5

[a]In the table, 100.0 indicates that in the absence of productivity change, real output would have suffered an absolute decline during 1950-70.

[b]The percentage increase 0.0 suggests that productivity change during 1950-70 was negative and would have reduced real output.

Source: See text.

TABLE 27

PERCENTAGE INCREASE IN REAL PRODUCT DURING 1950-70 DUE TO PRODUCTIVITY ADVANCE,

SOUTHEASTERN STATES

Economic Sector	Virginia	West Virginia	North Carolina	South Carolina	Georgia	Florida
Private Nonfarm	48.0%	100.0%	53.2%	56.4%	56.5%	36.2%
Mining	100.0[a]	100.0	90.3	62.1	76.8	80.6
Construction	0.0[a]	33.3	0.0	0.0	0.0	5.6
Manufacturing	53.7	100.0	64.4	64.3	64.2	55.1
Trade	47.4	83.0	42.7	58.7	50.3	40.6
Finance, Insurance and Real Estate	21.1	18.1	18.4	9.7	23.5	0.0
Transportation, Communication and Public Utilities	87.1	100.0	73.8	81.9	77.4	67.4
Services	0.4	6.0	4.4	24.3	37.5	0.0

Economic Sector	Kentucky	Tennessee	Alabama	Mississippi	Arkansas	Louisiana
Private Nonfarm	56.7%	51.0%	57.8%	52.5%	54.1%	59.6%
Mining	100.0	100.0	100.0	55.8	100.0	69.7
Construction	0.0	0.0	0.0	0.0	0.0	22.2
Manufacturing	55.1	53.7	69.4	62.9	61.6	82.5
Trade	48.9	53.5	48.3	51.6	52.6	52.5
Finance, Insurance and Real Estate	25.9	15.3	11.2	18.4	7.4	19.3
Transportation, Communication and Public Utilities	100.0	91.5	93.2	90.0	94.4	88.8
Services	0.0	11.0	0.0	0.0	0.0	0.0

[a]See notes to Table 26.

Source: See text.

occurred in West Virginia, which derived all of its increased output from improved labor efficiency. Within each area, industry variations were large. Mining, manufacturing, trade, transportation, communication, and public utilities were most dependent on productivity advance as a source of increase in real output. On the other hand, productivity advance was generally an unimportant source of growth in the construction, finance, insurance, real estate, and service industries.

Estimates of the impact of productivity change on per capita output growth can also be made. This involves summing the private nonfarm industry estimates of output that would have resulted in the absence of productivity change (Q_t^*) and adding to this total estimates of real product in government and agriculture. [9] Per capita output was recalculated, assuming no change in productivity, and these figures (PCQ_t^*) were compared with per capita output in the base period (PCQ_0) and the terminal year (PCQ_t). The estimated percentage increase in per capita output due to productivity change was calculated as follows:

$$(PCQ_t - PCQ_t^*/PCQ_t - PCQ_0)$$

These calculations appear in column (6) in table 28, and it is evident that the majority of per capita output advance during 1950-70 resulted from productivity change. The southeastern states derived approximately 60% of the increase in per capita output from efficiency improvements; on the other hand, the United States derived almost 80% of the increase in per capita output from increased efficiency in labor utilization. The calculations in column (4) in table 28 show the estimated real-dollar increases in per capita output that resulted from more efficient labor allocation during the past two decades. The magnitude of the absolute per capita output increases due to efficiency improvements emphasizes the crucial role of productivity change in our recent growth.

Recent thinking concerning the sources of American economic growth has identified a central theme claiming that growth is primarily the result of qualitative improvements in resource utilization. The empirical results obtained in this chapter by implementing

TABLE 28

PERCENTAGE INCREASE IN REAL PER CAPITA OUTPUT DURING 1950-70 DUE TO

PRODUCTIVITY ADVANCE, UNITED STATES, SOUTHEAST AND SOUTHEASTERN STATES

Area	(1) PCQ^*	(2) PCQ_{1970}	(3) PCQ_{1950}	(4) $PCQ_{1970}-PCQ^*$	(5) $PCQ_{1970}-PCQ_{1950}$	(6) Increase in PCQ Due to Productivity
United States	$2611	$3543	$2340	$932	$1203	77.5%
Southeast	2133	2957	1547	824	1410	58.4
Virginia	2459	3157	1922	698	1235	56.5
West Virginia	1987	3056	1832	1069	1224	87.3
North Carolina	2243	3211	1530	968	1681	57.6
South Carolina	1886	2695	1316	809	1379	58.7
Georgia	2102	3091	1515	989	1576	62.8
Florida	2325	3051	1925	726	1126	64.5
Kentucky	2238	3114	1551	876	1563	56.0
Tennessee	2204	2997	1556	793	1441	55.0
Alabama	1904	2632	1363	728	1269	57.4
Mississippi	1669	2295	992	626	1303	48.0
Arkansas	1854	2603	1112	749	1491	50.2
Louisiana	2042	2946	1738	904	1208	74.8

Source: See text.

Mills's concept of the productivity increment, which allows for segregation of the share of growth due to quantitative increases in the labor supply and qualitative improvements in the use of labor, corroborate the conclusions reached in earlier works. For the past two decades, productivity change has accounted for the major portion of national and southeastern growth in aggregate and per capita output.

VI. Why the Southeast Grows

To this point we have been concerned with the broad pattern of economic growth that occurred in the Southeast during the past two decades. To better understand the significance of this recent expansion and its consequences for the future, we need to take a closer look at the sources of past growth. Most analyses of the economic growth process focus on the goods-producing industries (manufacturing, mining, and agriculture) because these industries have the potential to produce a surplus for export. The output of the service industries (trade, finance, real estate, utilities, government, and others) is generally not exportable, and, in most instances, their growth is limited by the level and pace of development in the goods-producing sectors. Since manufacturing has been the primary growth sector in the American economy since the mid-nineteenth century, and because the data are readily available, most studies concerned with explaining regional economic growth concentrate on manufacturing developments.

The crucial importance of manufacturing to the southeastern economy has been shown in chapters II and III. During 1950-70, manufacturing was by far the leading source of growth in the Southeast, accounting for over one third of the total increase in real gross regional product. Between 1950 and 1970, in North Carolina, South Carolina, Kentucky, Tennessee, Alabama, Mississippi, Arkansas, and West Virginia, manufacturing accounted for 40% to 45% of the total increase in gross state product. In the remaining pages, I will attempt to summarize the findings of several major industrial location studies, and, in particular, I will point to the specific locational factors that have been responsible for the recent southeastern economic expansion. In addition to looking at the sources of industrial expansion during the recent past, some assessment will also be made of the prospects for continuation of the Southeast's economic progress.

FACTORS INVOLVED IN INDUSTRIAL LOCATION

The best-known and most widely cited studies of industrial location are those of Glenn McLaughlin and Stefan Robock, Victor Fuchs, and Harvey Perloff, Edgar Dunn, Eric Lampard, and Richard Muth (cited as Perloff et al.).[1] The McLaughlin and Robock and Perloff et al. studies suggested that access to markets, labor cost and availability, and supplies of materials and resources were the most important factors in choosing a location.[2] Industries that produce high-weight final products (automobiles) are generally concerned with market and transportation factors; labor-intensive industries (textiles, apparel) are generally motivated by labor costs and availability; and resource-intensive industries (paper, lumber) are restricted to locations offering the required materials. McLaughlin and Robock's study of eighty-eight plants that moved to the South during the late 1940s suggested that 45% of the plants were oriented primarily to markets, 30% were oriented to materials and resources, and 25% were oriented to labor.[3] In addition to the major forces of markets, labor, and materials, the following secondary influences on location decisions are often considered: taxes, climate, living conditions, availability of plant sites, management personnel, capital, and other factors that vary by state and region. The work of Fuchs is in agreement with these other studies in suggesting that labor and raw materials have played a significant role in the regional pattern of industrial location; however, the importance of markets in regional location is questioned.[4]

A recent study by Leonard Wheat provides an excellent synthesis of areas of conflict and agreement in these and other studies and also provides an assessment of factors behind regional manufacturing growth during 1947-63.[5] Wheat argues that markets and climate were of primary importance, labor cost and availability and thresholds (prior levels of development) were of secondary importance, and resources, urbanization, and agglomeration were relatively insignificant.[6] Table 29 reproduces Wheat's summary results on the explanatory power of the various locational factors for absolute and per capita manufacturing growth during 1947-63. Wheat's results put much more emphasis on climate than any other study, but they also show the importance of markets, labor, and resources. An excellent summary of responses gathered in numerous questionnaire and interview surveys regarding factors underlying location decisions is provided by William Morgan.[7] Both the questionnaire and interview results suggest that the primary forces behind industrial location decisions are markets, labor, and raw materials.

TABLE 29

PERCENTAGE OF ABSOLUTE AND PER CAPITA GROWTH IN MANUFACTURING

DURING 1947-63 EXPLAINED BY VARIOUS

LOCATION FACTORS

Location Factor	Absolute Growth	Per Capita Growth
Markets	65%	45%
Climate	21	22
Labor	6	11
Thresholds[a]	3	10
Resources	4	8
Urban Attraction	1	4

[a]Thresholds refer to prior levels of development.

Source: Wheat, Regional Growth, Table 7-5, p. 209.

Many locational studies have focused attention on the recent industrial boom in the South. A study by the Fantus Company concerned with industrialization in the Appalachian region concluded that the most important factors influencing plant location decisions were the following: transportation, proximity to customers, state manpower training assistance, labor-cost advantages, low-cost electrical power, urban orientation, and proximity to raw materials. [8] Transportation and nearness to customers both reflect market considerations; manpower assistance and labor cost are both aspects of the labor supply problem; and electric power and materials reflect the resource advantages of a region. A detailed survey of 5,000 plants that expanded or located in the South during 1956-60 was conducted by Thomas Bergin and William Eagan. [9] The most important factors in choosing a southern location were markets, labor, and raw materials. A study of location decisions of plants that located in Georgia during the postwar period stressed the importance of markets and labor, and a study of location decisions of Florida plants stressed the crucial role of markets. [10]

THE ROLE OF MARKETS

Market factors are intended to capture the advantages of a location resulting from nearness to consumer markets. This involves not only availability of consumer demand but also adequate transportation facilities to tap existing markets for the final product. Agglomeration effects, such as external economies resulting from concentration of industry, are difficult to separate from market effects because many firms produce for the industrial market rather than the consumer market. For example, a market-oriented industry such as automobile production may locate near significant consumer markets but this may also attract subsidiary industries that produce goods for the automobile industry such as electrical machinery and fabricated metals.

It is the consensus of most studies that markets have been the most significant factor in the Southeast's recent progress. Not only does the Southeast have ready access through interstate highways, ocean shipping, railroads, and air transportation to the major consumer markets in the Northeast, but the southeastern consumer market is also expanding at a rapid rate. McLaughlin and Robock cited rising income in the Southeast as the most important factor behind the rise of new industry in the region. [11] Evidence of this expanding market within the South is provided in table 30, which shows relative per capita income trends in the Southeast during 1929-72. During this period, the Southeast moved from 52% of parity with the national standard in 1929 to 85% in 1972. Despite the tremendous relative improvement in the Southeast's standard of living, the region still lags behind national welfare standards, and, according to the 1970 census, 16% of all southerners were below the poverty level compared to 8% of all nonsoutherners. [12] However, because of the circular relationship between industrial growth and per capita income improvement, continuation of recent growth trends should eliminate the gap between national and southeastern per capita income levels. New industry in the Southeast bids labor away from less productive industries and provides employment in better paying occupations. The increased employment in higher paying occupations creates a rise in per capita income and this attracts market oriented manufacturing industries and creates a demand for services and other activities. The high rate of recent expansion in the Southeast highlighted in earlier chapters and reflected in the per capita income relatives in table 30 should insure that the Southeast will continue to expand and attract market oriented industries.

THE ROLE OF LABOR

Next to markets, the most often mentioned factor underlying recent southeastern expansion is labor. It has long been recognized that the Southeast is characterized by low-cost labor, and this is a definite attraction to industries with labor-intensive production techniques. However, responses to questionnaire and interview surveys show that managers are concerned with more than the cost of labor. They are also interested in the availability of labor supplies, quality of labor, strength of unions, right-to-work laws, turnover, absenteeism, fringe benefits, and other factors. In general, low wages, weak unions, and surplus labor provided a strong inducement to labor-oriented industries. If low-cost labor is available in abundance, firms can be selective in choosing their employees and can obtain labor without pushing up wages. Unions have a positive effect on wage rates, and they also bring an organization and set of regulations that management often prefers to avoid.

TABLE 30

PER CAPITA INCOME IN THE SOUTHEAST AND THE SOUTHEASTERN STATES

RELATIVE TO THE NATIONAL AVERAGE, 1929-72

(United States = 100)

State or Region	1929	1940	1950	1960	1970	1972
Virginia	62	78	82	83	93	96
West Virginia	66	68	71	73	77	80
North Carolina	48	55	69	70	82	85
South Carolina	38	52	60	62	75	77
Georgia	50	57	69	74	84	87
Florida	74	86	86	88	94	97
Kentucky	56	54	66	71	79	80
Tennessee	54	57	66	70	78	82
Alabama	46	47	59	68	74	76
Mississippi	41	37	50	54	66	70
Arkansas	43	43	55	62	73	79
Louisiana	59	61	75	75	78	75
Southeast	52	58	68	73	82	85

Source: The 1929 and 1940 figures are from the U.S. Department of Commerce, Personal Income by States Since 1929 (Washington: Government Printing Office, 1955); the 1950-72 figures are from the U.S. Departmen of Commerce, Survey of Current Business, August 1973.

The recent industrial boom in the Southeast has had very little impact on the relative cost advantage of southern labor. Table 31 shows 1954 and 1970 wages per manhour for production workers in the two-digit manufacturing industry categories for the United States, non-South, South Atlantic, East South Central, and West South Central regions. [13] Table 32 shows the parity between southern wages and the national average for 1954 and 1970. It is clear from both sets of data that there has been very little change in the cost position of southern labor vis-à-vis national labor during the past two decades.

TABLE 31

AVERAGE COST PER MANHOUR FOR PRODUCTION WORKERS, BY TWO-DIGIT MANUFACTURING INDUSTRY, UNITED STATES,

NON-SOUTH, SOUTH ATLANTIC, EAST SOUTH CENTRAL, AND WEST SOUTH CENTRAL REGIONS, 1954 AND 1970

		1954			
SIC Code Number and Industry	United States	Non-South	South Atlantic	East South Central	West South Central
20 Food	$1.62	$1.73	$1.22	$1.35	$1.28
21 Tobacco	1.35	1.27	1.38	1.41	1.04
22 Textiles	1.39	1.56	1.28	1.23	1.16
23 Apparel	1.33	1.42	1.07	.97	1.00
24 Lumber	1.45	1.80	.99	.99	1.03
25 Furniture	1.56	1.73	1.21	1.19	1.25
26 Paper	1.80	1.82	1.73	1.75	1.78
27 Printing and Publishing	2.20	2.26	1.92	1.89	1.79
28 Chemicals	1.97	2.01	1.83	1.90	2.07
29 Petroleum and Coal Products	2.41	2.39	2.18	2.09	2.52
30 Rubber	2.05	2.07	1.59	2.14	2.07
31 Leather	1.42	1.44	1.30	1.22	1.13
32 Stone, Clay and Glass	1.81	1.89	1.56	1.48	1.55
33 Primary Metals	2.20	2.22	2.18	2.04	2.03
34 Fabricated Metals	1.92	1.95	1.71	1.69	1.68
35 Non-electrical Machinery	2.10	2.13	1.65	1.84	1.85
36 Electrical Machinery	1.86	1.87	1.71	1.55	1.53
37 Transportation Equipment	2.21	2.22	2.11	2.02	2.15
38 Instruments	1.94	1.96	1.47	1.77	1.55
39 Miscellaneous	1.71	1.73	1.41	1.56	1.56
Total	1.83	1.93	1.43	1.47	1.66

		1970			
SIC Code Number and Industry	United States	Non-South	South Atlantic	East South Central	West South Central
20 Food	$3.17	$3.41	$2.54	$2.64	$2.58
21 Tobacco	3.05	2.75	3.21	- -	- -
22 Textiles	2.48	2.62	2.44	2.32	2.35
23 Apparel	2.24	2.38	2.06	1.99	1.98
24 Lumber	2.77	3.15	2.22	2.19	2.20
25 Furniture	2.69	3.10	2.35	2.23	2.24
26 Paper	3.56	3.53	3.54	3.78	3.66
27 Printing and Publishing	3.89	4.02	3.57	3.27	3.16
28 Chemicals	3.86	3.84	3.66	3.76	4.47
29 Petroleum and Coal Products	4.56	4.53	3.51	3.90	4.77
30 Rubber	3.25	3.31	2.74	3.25	3.20
31 Leather	2.47	2.49	2.22	- -	- -
32 Stone, Clay and Glass	3.50	3.66	3.08	3.18	3.08
33 Primary Metals	4.18	4.23	4.15	3.96	3.62
34 Fabricated Metals	3.56	3.68	2.86	3.03	3.29
35 Non-electrical Machinery	3.88	4.00	3.07	3.39	3.24
36 Electrical Machinery	3.41	3.52	3.01	2.84	3.05
37 Transportation Equipment	4.27	4.41	3.90	3.41	3.72
38 Instruments	3.45	3.56	2.72	2.26	2.90
39 Miscellaneous	2.72	2.78	2.36	2.27	2.37
Total	3.42	3.63	2.78	2.85	3.13

Source: U.S. Bureau of the Census, Census of Manufactures, 1954 and Annual Survey of Manufactures, 1970.

TABLE 32

AVERAGE COST PER MANHOUR FOR PRODUCTION WORKERS IN THE SOUTHERN REGIONS RELATIVE TO THE NATIONAL

AVERAGE, 1954 AND 1970

(United States = 100)

SIC Code Number and Industry	1954			1970		
	South Atlantic	East South Central	West South Central	South Atlantic	East South Central	West South Central
20 Food	75.3	83.3	79.0	80.1	83.3	81.4
21 Tobacco	102.2	104.4	77.0	105.3	- -	- -
22 Textiles	92.1	88.5	83.5	98.4	93.6	94.8
23 Apparel	80.5	72.9	75.2	92.0	88.8	88.4
24 Lumber	68.3	68.3	71.0	80.1	79.1	79.4
25 Furniture	77.6	76.3	80.1	87.4	82.9	83.3
26 Paper	96.1	97.2	98.9	99.4	106.2	102.8
27 Printing and Publishing	87.3	85.9	81.4	91.8	84.1	81.2
28 Chemicals	92.9	96.5	105.1	94.8	97.4	115.8
29 Petroleum and Coal Products	90.5	86.7	104.6	77.0	85.5	104.6
30 Rubber	77.6	104.4	101.0	84.3	100.0	98.5
31 Leather	91.6	85.9	79.6	89.9	- -	- -
32 Stone, Clay and Glass	86.2	81.2	85.6	88.0	90.0	88.0
33 Primary Metals	99.1	92.7	92.3	99.3	94.7	86.6
34 Fabricated Metals	89.1	88.0	87.5	80.3	85.1	92.4
35 Non-electrical Machinery	78.6	87.6	88.1	79.1	87.4	83.5
36 Electrical Machinery	91.9	83.3	82.3	88.3	83.3	89.4
37 Transportation Equipment	95.5	91.4	97.3	91.3	79.9	87.1
38 Instruments	75.8	91.2	79.9	78.8	65.5	84.1
39 Miscellaneous	82.5	91.2	91.2	86.8	83.5	87.1
Total	78.1	80.3	90.7	81.3	83.3	91.5

Source: Computed from Table 31.

I have also examined median earnings by major occupation for all industries in the South and the United States. The results in table 33 indicate that occupational earnings are lower in the South than in the nation, especially for males. In general, male earnings in the South are closer to parity with the national average for the more highly skilled occupations; the greatest discrepancy occurs in the relatively low-skilled occupations of farmers, laborers, operatives, and service workers. Female earnings in the South are relatively close to the national standard in most occupations.

In addition to being relatively low cost, the South's labor supply is also characterized by a relatively low degree of unionization, although regional differences have narrowed in recent decades. In 1970, the percentage of the nation's nonagricultural employment with union membership stood at 27.9%; the following unionized shares were shown in the southeastern states: Virginia, 16.7%; West Virginia, 43.0%; North Carolina, 7.8%; South Carolina, 9.6%; Georgia, 16.2%; Florida, 13.9%; Kentucky, 27.3%; Tennessee, 20.6%; Alabama, 20.3%; Mississippi, 13.2%; Arkansas, 17.9%; and Louisiana, 18.4%. [14] An analysis of the number of mandays idle for

TABLE 33

MEDIAN EARNINGS IN THE SOUTH RELATIVE TO THE NATIONAL

AVERAGE, BY MAJOR OCCUPATION AND SEX, 1970

(United States = 100)

Occupation Group	Males	Females
Professional, technical and kindred workers	91.9	94.9
Managers and administrators, except farm	87.7	90.8
Sales workers	90.3	103.3
Clerical and kindred workers	91.6	94.8
Craftsmen and kindred workers	85.1	90.5
Operatives, except transport	81.7	93.0
Transport equipment operatives	79.1	91.9
Laborers, except farm	77.2	93.7
Farmers and farm managers	75.2	92.1
Farm laborers and farm foremen	88.7	83.5
Service workers, except private household	81.5	94.1
Private household workers	86.5	95.1
Total experienced civilian labor force	84.5	91.9

Source: U.S. Bureau of the Census, Census of the United States: 1970, Detailed Characteristics, United States Summary, Tables 227, 228, 296, and 297.

nonagricultural labor in the South and non-South during 1969-71 reveals no substantial regional difference in work stoppages. [15]

A negative factor for the Southeast on the labor side is the relatively low quality of southern labor as reflected in educational attainment. The results from questionnaires and other surveys indicate that many managers believe that much southern labor is of low quality. However, McLaughlin and Robock's study points out that plants with southern and nonsouthern locations found southern labor to be of similar productivity. [16] It is clear from educational statistics that the average southerner has less formal education than individuals in other regions. [17] It has also been true that the quality of southern education has been relatively low.

Information regarding the quantity of education is available from the census, and table 34 shows median years of school completed, by age, sex, and race in 1970. The recent improvement of the South in the quantity of education is clear in the figures. For those between

TABLE 34

MEDIAN YEARS OF COMPLETED EDUCATION, UNITED STATES AND SOUTH, BY

AGE, RACE, AND SEX, 1970

Age Group	All Males		Negro Males		All Females		Negro Females	
	U.S.	South	U.S.	South	U.S.	South	U.S.	South
20-24	12.7	12.6	12.2	12.1	12.6	12.5	12.3	12.3
25-29	12.6	12.5	12.1	11.8	12.5	12.4	12.2	12.0
30-34	12.5	12.4	11.7	10.9	12.4	12.3	11.9	11.3
35-39	12.4	12.2	11.0	10.0	12.3	12.2	11.4	10.7
40-44	12.2	11.9	10.1	8.9	12.3	12.0	10.8	10.0
45-49	12.2	11.4	9.3	8.2	12.2	11.7	10.0	9.0
50-54	12.0	10.7	8.5	7.4	12.1	11.1	9.0	8.3
55-59	10.7	9.5	7.6	6.5	11.1	10.3	8.4	7.7
60-64	9.6	8.8	6.9	5.9	10.4	9.6	7.9	7.2
25 and over	12.1	11.2	9.4	8.2	12.1	11.4	10.1	9.0

Source: U.S. Bureau of the Census, Census of the United States: 1970, Detailed Characteristics, United States Summary, Tables 199 and 276.

the ages of twenty and twenty-nine in each sex and racial group, there was virtually no difference between the South and the nation in median years of completed education. Information regarding the quality of southern education is available from performance on the Armed Forces Qualification Test. In 1970, 5.7% of all selective service draftees in the nation failed to qualify for military service because of mental deficiencies. The following failure rates were reported for draftees from southeastern states: Virginia, 9.1%; West Virginia, 5.9%; North Carolina, 12.7%; South Carolina, 22.3%; Georgia, 14.3%; Florida, 6.7%; Kentucky, 5.3%; Tennessee, 6.0%; Alabama, 11.0%; Mississippi, 19.2%; Arkansas, 8.1%; and Louisiana, 11.8%. [18] Further information regarding the quality of education is available from the Coleman Report, which also pointed to the low quality of southern education. [19] Table 35 summarizes the findings of the Coleman Report regarding regional and racial variation in performance on achievement tests. It is clear from the figures that the average quality of a high school degree from a southern school in 1965 was below the national standard and in most cases below the average for any other region. [20]

The Coleman Report data are almost a decade old and recent improvements in southern education do not show up in the figures. However, it is likely that the South still has a relatively undereducated labor force. Many advances have been made during the past two decades but substantial grounds for improvement remain. Southern school teachers are still among the lowest-paid educators in

TABLE 35

GRADE LEVELS BEHIND THE AVERAGE WHITE IN THE METROPOLITAN

NORTHEAST WITH 12 YEARS OF EDUCATION, BY VERBAL

ABILITY, READING COMPREHENSION, AND MATH

ACHIEVEMENT, 1965

Race and Area	Verbal Ability	Reading Comprehension	Math Achievement
White, Nonmetro			
South	1.5	1.0	1.4
Southwest	0.8	0.5	0.8
North	0.9	0.5	0.8
White, Metro			
Northeast	0.0	0.0	0.0
Midwest	0.4	0.3	0.1
South	0.9	0.4	1.2
Southwest	0.7	0.4	0.6
West	0.5	0.8	0.8
Negro, Nonmetro			
South	5.2	4.9	6.2
Southwest	4.7	4.5	5.6
North	4.2	3.8	5.2
Negro, Metro			
Northeast	3.3	2.9	5.2
Midwest	3.3	2.8	4.7
South	4.2	3.9	5.6
Southwest	4.3	4.1	5.7
West	3.9	3.8	5.3

Source: Joseph S. Coleman et al, Equality of Educational Opportunity (Washington, D.C.: U.S. Department of Health, Education, and Welfare, Office of Education, 1966), pp. 274-75.

the nation, and expenditures per pupil in the Southeast are markedly below the national average.[21] Recent studies by Maddox et al. and Colberg have argued that qualitative improvement of the southern labor force is a requirement for continued expansion and prosperity of the region.[22]

The ability of low southern wages to draw industry to the South has been questioned by several authors. Calvin Hoover and B. U. Ratchford argued that industrialists are more concerned with access to markets, materials, and dependability of the labor supply than they are with wage rates. Future prospects for the wage differential are difficult to predict in light of increases in the minimum wage and increased unionization in the South. [23] It is also argued that technological change is working to create increased demand for highly skilled labor and that future demand for unskilled low-wage labor is uncertain. [24]

Wheat's analysis indicated that labor was an important factor in location decisions only for labor-intensive industries. [25] Among the labor variables he studied, wages were found to be the most significant, labor surplus was found to have some significance, and strength of unions was found to be rather insignificant. Wheat's analysis showed that labor-oriented industries seek locations with low wages, particularly the South. The concentration of low-wage industries in an area such as the Southeast perpetuates the low-income status of the region and does not attract market-oriented industries. Wheat suggests that the effects of cheap labor may be offsetting, and the net effect may be insignificant. Wheat's argument overlooks the fact that the initial movement of low-wage manufacturing industries to the Southeast offered higher wage employment than agriculture. Despite the low-wage character of many labor-intensive industries relative to other manufacturing, the rise of these industries in the Southeast resulted in a substantial increase in the region's income and market attractiveness. However, if the Southeast concentrated only on low-wage labor-intensive manufacturing industries, a ceiling would be placed on the region's income, and this would adversely influence its market potential.

Studies of industrial location by Perloff et al. and Fuchs suggested that the South's recent industrial expansion included gains in both labor and nonlabor intensive industries. Perloff et al., using capital/labor ratios, separated the two-digit manufacturing industries into labor-intensive (electrical and nonelectrical machinery, printing and publishing, textiles, lumber, furniture, transportation equipment excluding motor vehicles, leather and leather products, and apparel) and capital-intensive (petroleum and coal products, chemicals, motor vehicles, tobacco, and paper and paper products). [26] Fuchs measured labor intensity by computing the ratio of wages paid to production workers/value added. The labor-intensive industries were separated into low wage (textile, apparel, lumber, furniture, leather, stone, clay, glass, and miscellaneous manufacturing) and high wage (rubber, primary metals, fabricated metals, machinery, and transportation equipment). [27] Fuchs found that during the 1930s and 1940s the South Atlantic and East South Central states made larger gains in low-wage, nonlabor-intensive industries (food, tobacco, pulp, and paper) than they did in low-wage labor-intensive industries. At the same time, the West South Central states made their greatest gains in high-wage labor-intensive industries. [28]

TABLE 36

SOUTHEAST'S PERCENTAGE DISTRIBUTION OF MANUFACTURING VALUE ADDED AND PERCENTAGE

SHARES OF NATIONAL VALUE ADDED, BY TWO-DIGIT INDUSTRY, 1954 AND 1970

SIC Code Number and Industry	1954		1970	
	Percentage Distribution	Shares of National Value Added	Percentage Distribution	Shares of National Value Added
20 Food	12.6%	13.7%	10.6%	17.4%
21 Tobacco	5.4	80.0	4.8	90.0
22 Textiles	16.1	49.6	12.1	68.6
23 Apparel	4.3	12.3	5.9	26.4
24 Lumber	5.5	25.3	3.3	29.2
25 Furniture	2.7	20.1	3.1	33.3
26 Paper	7.0	22.3	5.9	27.0
27 Printing and Publishing	3.1	7.3	3.7	11.2
28 Chemicals	15.2	23.4	13.9	26.0
29 Petroleum and Coal Products	2.3	13.2	1.6	15.2
30 Rubber	1.0	8.0	2.6	16.4
31 Leather	0.9	6.9	0.9	16.7
32 Stone, Clay and Glass	3.7	14.1	3.6	19.2
33 Primary Metals	5.6	8.8	4.5	10.9
34 Fabricated Metals	3.8	7.2	4.3	10.7
35 Non-electrical Machinery	2.7	3.2	5.2	8.6
36 Electrical Machinery	1.9	3.7	7.0	13.1
37 Transportation Equipment	4.5	4.7	5.4	9.8
38 Instruments	0.2	1.7	0.7	4.7
39 Miscellaneous	1.5	4.7	1.1	10.3
Total		12.5		17.5

Source: U.S. Bureau of the Census, Census of Manufactures, 1954 and Annual Survey of Manufactures, 1970.

I have examined structural changes in southeastern manufacturing during the period 1954-70, and the results show a great deal of balance in the region's recent expansion. The two-digit industrial composition of southeastern manufacturing and the industry shares of national value added are shown in table 36 for 1954 and 1970. The figures are clear and are left for the interested reader to evaluate. I have also calculated the percentage contribution of each two-digit industry to the real change in southeastern value added during 1954-70.[29] (See table 37.) Using Perloff et al.'s definition of labor and capital-intensive manufacturing, I estimated that 46.5% of industrial expansion during 1954-70 occurred in labor-intensive industries and 29.6% occurred in capital-intensive industries.[30] Using Fuchs's definitions, I estimated that 28.8% of the recent industrial growth occurred in low-wage labor-intensive industries, 30.9% occurred in high-wage labor-intensive industries, and 40.3% occurred in non-

TABLE 37

TWO-DIGIT INDUSTRY PERCENTAGE SHARES OF ABSOLUTE GAIN IN REAL

MANUFACTURING VALUE ADDED, 1954-70

SIC Code Number and Industry	% Share of Absolute Gain in Value Added
20 Food	8.7%
21 Tobacco	3.6
22 Textiles	11.4
23 Apparel	7.1
24 Lumber	2.0
25 Furniture	3.5
26 Paper	5.4
27 Printing and Publishing	4.0
28 Chemicals	16.4
29 Petroleum and Coal Products	1.3
30 Rubber	3.8
31 Leather	0.7
32 Stone, Clay and Glass	3.3
33 Primary Metals	2.8
34 Fabricated Metals	3.6
35 Non-electrical Machinery	5.7
36 Electrical Machinery	10.1
37 Transportation Equipment	4.9
38 Instruments	0.9
39 Miscellaneous	0.8
Total	100.0

Source: See text.

labor-intensive industries. It appears that cheap labor in the Southeast has not restricted the region's development to concentration on labor-intensive industries. Instead, recent trends show a broadening of the Southeast's industrial base to include heavy emphasis on a variety of different types of manufacturing.

THE ROLE OF RESOURCES AND RAW MATERIALS

Resources and raw materials have had an important influence on the location of several southeastern industries. The food processing, lumber, pulp and paper, chemicals, tobacco, primary metals, and the stone, clay, and glass industries are all heavily dependent on adequate supplies of local materials. The South's vast forest resources, mineral wealth, food surpluses, water resources, and energy resources have accounted for a substantial portion of the growth in these materials-oriented industries. Wheat suggests that no one region has a monopoly on resource advantages, and, therefore, he downplays their importance in industrial location decisions. [31] However, where particular resources have been concentrated, industries have located to exploit the resource base. Perloff et al., Fuchs, Hoover and Ratchford, and McLaughlin and Robock all point to the Southeast's availability of resources as a major factor in the region's industrial development. In addition to having abundant materials and energy resources, the Southeast has large supplies of available land for industrial expansion. Fuchs points to land availability as a factor in the trend toward large one-story plants that permit more efficient operation than multistory units. [32]

The Southeast's most important resource advantages appear to be in forest products and energy supplies. Data on forest land, current output of sawtimber, and current growing stock show that the South accounts for almost 40% of the nation's current sawtimber production and growing stock of hardwoods. The region's share of the nation's softwoods is much smaller, with most concentrated in the West. [33] The South's power and energy reserves are substantial. It is estimated that the region presently contains approximately 60% of all undeveloped water resources and approximately 60% of all developed and undeveloped conventional hydroelectric power in the eastern United States. [34] Abundant low-cost power has been one of the Southeast's major resource advantages over the Northeast, and table 38 exhibits representative electrical rates for low-usage (15,000 kwh) and high-usage (30,000kwh) customers in 1966. It is clear that most southern locations have a distinct cost advantage in electrical power over northeastern and mid-western sites.

Most locational studies separate climate from natural resources and materials and view it as an independent factor. Regardless of how climate is viewed, there appears to be some consensus that climate alone has been a significant factor in the Southeast's growth. The Southeast's climate assures year-round operation in outdoor industries, guarantees transportation, and allows cheaper plant operation and maintenance costs. The region's weather has also attracted military bases to the area, and these establishments have provided a stimulus to local consumer demand. Before the development of air conditioning, the summer heat was considered a locational disadvantage for the Southeast. Now, with air-conditioned plants, offices, homes, and automobiles, the summer heat is no longer a negative factor, and the mild climate acts as a positive force in the region's development. In addition to being attractive to industry, the climate encourages in-migration of retirees which augments the region's consumer demand. Locational studies by Perloff et al. and Fuchs stress the importance of climate in the location of the aircraft industry and military bases and as an influence on migration patterns. [35]

TAXES AND FINANCIAL INDUCEMENTS

One remaining group of factors that have been considered in many locational studies and that have been found to be of little significance are state and local influences such as taxes and financial inducements. The South, more than any other region, has catered to industry through low taxes and financial inducements. Morgan has made a detailed study of the impact of these factors on industrial location decisions, particularly with regard to location decisions in the South. [36] He concluded that tax costs, tax concessions, and other financial inducements were not a significant locational determinant. Other recent studies have arrived at similar conclusions. [37]

CAPITAL

Local capital supplies have not been considered an important factor in industrial location decisions because of the existence of a national capital market in the United States. As a result, the Southeast's low-income status is not considered to be a significant obstacle to the region's development. The establishment of branch plants with headquarters outside the Southeast and the general mobility of capital in

the nation have overcome the region's deficiency of indigenous capital supplies. [38]

TABLE 38

AVERAGE CHARGE IN CENTS PER KILOWATT-HOUR, 1966, SELECTED CITIES

City	Low Usage (15,000 kwh)	High Usage (30,000 kwh)
Birmingham, Alabama	1.40	1.30
Los Angeles, California	1.36	1.30
Bridgeport, Connecticut	1.73	1.64
Wilmington, Delaware	1.80	1.64
Orlando, Florida	1.87	1.68
Atlanta, Georgia	1.38	1.29
Chicago, Illinois	1.57	1.39
Indianapolis, Indiana	1.46	1.28
New Orleans, Louisiana	1.70	1.52
Baltimore, Maryland	1.66	1.43
Boston, Massachusetts	2.05	1.92
Detroit, Michigan	1.68	1.53
Jackson, Mississippi	1.25	1.05
St. Louis, Missouri	1.66	1.56
Newark, New Jersey	1.67	1.48
New York, New York	2.00	1.74
Greensboro, North Carolina	1.53	1.31
Cincinnati, Ohio	1.75	1.53
Portland, Oregon	1.07	1.07
Philadelphia, Pennsylvania	1.75	1.74
Providence, Rhode Island	2.02	1.88
Charleston, South Carolina	1.63	1.44
Memphis, Tennessee	0.84	0.75
Houston, Texas	1.57	1.40
Richmond, Virginia	1.61	1.41

Source: U.S. Federal Power Commission, All Electric Homes, 1966.

PROSPECTS FOR THE FUTURE

This study has surveyed recent southeastern ecoomic growth and has
shown that the region's expansion has been broadly based, involving
substantial increases in industrialization as well as in the service-
producing industries, particularly finance, insurance, real estate,
and wholesale and retail trade. The prospects for continuation of this
cumulative growth process are very encouraging. The recent growth
of the Southeast has resulted in rapidly expanding markets that act to
draw market-oriented industries to the region. The Southeast is also
favored by its proximity to the major consumer markets in the Northeast, its abundant supplies of relatively low-cost labor and energy,

and its abundant supply of untapped resources. In addition to these favorable economic signs, recent improvements in race relations and the breakdown of racial discrimination in the South suggest that in the future the region will make more efficient use of all its resources.

This does not mean to suggest that the region does not face problems in the future. Despite significant progress in the past two decades, there is still much racial discrimination in the South. However, recent evidence is encouraging and suggests that the rate of progress in improving race relations has been faster in the South than in the rest of the nation. [39] Another crucial requirement for the Southeast's future growth is the continued upgrading of the region's human resources. Educational improvements during the past two decades have been substantial, but the quality of southern education is still decidedly below the national norm. Improved education will allow the South to compete more vigorously with other regions for all types of economic activity and to make the most of its market, resource, and climatic advantages.

At the outset, I indicated that this study was motivated by the lack of comprehensive data series that could serve as the basis for analysis of state and regional economic growth. In this work, I have attempted to correct this deficiency for the Southeast region and the individual southeastern states. The carefully prepared historical gross state product series presented in this study has allowed many insights into the dimensions and industrial sources of the Southeast's recent economic expansion. Previously existing data sources would not have allowed for this thorough examination.

In surveying recent growth trends in the Southeast region and in the southeastern states, the above chapters suggest that the future growth prospects for the Southeast are very promising. However, the examination of growth trends was restricted to the major issues, and it is hoped that this author's effort to correct data deficiencies is put to additional use. The data provided in the statistical appendix represent an invaluable research tool for anyone interested in state and regional development, the southeastern economy, and particular southeastern states. The estimates contained in the appendix tables can support further research efforts aimed at expanding our comprehension of the process of recent southeastern economic growth; they can also provide a basis for forecasting future patterns of growth. The data bank in the appendix also provides a solid basis for continuous updating of gross state product estimates for the individual southeastern states. It is hoped that the task of extending the estimates provided in this study is taken up by other researchers concerned with state and regional economic development. As gross state product estimates become available for other states and later time periods, additional analyses will become possible, and these can further improve our knowledge and understanding of the process of state and regional economic growth.

Appendix Tables
Notes
Bibliography
Index

Appendix Tables

The data presented in the following tables represent this author's attempt to reconstruct the recent statistical past of the Southeast region and the individual southeastern states. As outlined in chapter I, the model used to generate the gross product estimates is subject to several sources of bias. The most crucial assumption is that, within given industries, the factor proportions in the nation and in all states are similar. This assumption is avoided in agriculture, and an adjustment of the manufacturing estimates is made in order to reduce the influence of this assumption. The other major assumption is that, for given industries, price movements during the past two decades have been similar in the nation and in all states.

The rationale for making these assumptions and the potential source of bias introduced by the model are treated fully in chapter I, and it is suggested that the reader carefully review this chapter before attempting to use the appendix data. The author feels that the estimates contained in this study are the most accurate and thorough survey of recent economic development in the Southeast. However, one should be fully aware of the limitations of the estimates before using them for analysis.

Appendix Tables

APPENDIX TABLE I

GROSS REGIONAL PRODUCT, SOUTHEAST, 1950-70

(Millions of Dollars)

Economic Sector	1950	1951	1952	1953	1954	1955	1956
Mining	1961.1	2139.1	2125.0	1950.5	1850.0	2186.1	2531.0
Construction	1902.9	2435.8	2972.6	2971.2	2661.4	2711.8	3087.5
Manufacturing	11326.6	13065.9	13048.5	14211.2	13566.5	16893.8	17557.5
Trade	7261.9	8080.7	8824.5	8852.0	9018.0	9922.6	10783.1
Finance, Insurance and Real Estate	3629.8	4077.8	4593.7	5194.4	5678.1	6171.7	6819.5
Transportation, Communication and Public Utilities	3834.3	4407.5	4783.2	4963.6	4988.9	5421.8	5949.4
Services	3583.2	4052.7	4312.3	4613.3	4789.6	5413.6	6105.5
Government	4337.0	5886.7	6744.5	6933.2	6983.5	7238.0	7621.3
Farm	4488.3	5399.5	5079.2	4931.9	4357.3	4903.8	4523.8
Total	42325.1	49545.7	52483.5	54621.3	53893.3	60863.2	64978.7

Economic Sector	1957	1958	1959	1960	1961	1962	1963
Mining	2622.2	2313.8	2352.7	2398.0	2352.1	2377.7	2461.2
Construction	3363.1	3347.4	3583.5	3569.0	3584.1	3886.6	4253.7
Manufacturing	18161.4	17798.5	19864.6	20507.2	20950.1	23558.4	25053.9
Trade	11346.7	11526.8	12587.0	12887.8	13250.5	14330.0	15180.2
Finance, Insurance and Real Estate	7461.8	7949.0	8764.1	9355.5	9854.4	10668.5	11470.3
Transportation, Communication and Public Utilities	6330.5	6407.4	6914.4	7207.5	7501.4	8028.0	8504.3
Service	6630.0	6950.9	7526.3	7461.9	8376.2	9051.2	9808.6
Government	8333.4	8869.9	9378.8	9884.7	10680.9	11708.2	12609.5
Farm	3859.8	4449.3	4720.6	4670.4	5133.7	5056.0	5472.6
Total	68108.9	69613.0	75692.0	77942.0	81683.4	88664.6	94814.3

Economic Sector	1964	1965	1966	1967	1968	1969	1970
Mining	2531.9	2725.1	2807.0	2876.0	2974.6	3262.4	3563.8
Construction	4758.6	5511.9	6371.4	6650.1	7240.3	8161.2	8537.9
Manufacturing	27418.1	30445.0	34267.0	35373.1	40682.0	41367.8	46326.8
Trade	16612.3	18016.4	19997.5	21580.5	23885.0	26461.8	28727.7
Finance, Insurance and Real Estate	12417.4	13736.2	14935.0	16078.6	17407.4	19202.6	20808.6
Transportation, Communication and Public Utilities	9257.7	9932.7	10857.7	11450.8	12581.8	13629.7	14560.1
Services	10829.0	11855.4	12387.4	13606.1	14971.6	17247.9	19113.3
Government	13768.5	14831.0	16716.3	18865.3	20951.0	22850.8	25073.5
Farm	5453.2	5404.0	5495.7	5544.8	5735.9	6503.3	6459.6
Total	103046.7	112457.7	123835.0	132025.3	146429.6	158687.5	173171.3

Appendix Tables

APPENDIX TABLE II

REAL GROSS REGIONAL PRODUCT, SOUTHEAST, 1950-70

(Millions of 1958 Dollars)

Economic Sector	1950	1951	1952	1953	1954	1955	1956
Mining	2280.3	2473.0	2442.7	2226.5	1991.5	2286.8	2566.8
Construction	2433.5	2967.0	3366.4	3375.3	3073.1	3131.4	3367.1
Manufacturing	14263.6	15389.5	15049.2	16313.0	15260.0	18666.4	18559.3
Trade	8543.4	8792.7	9488.7	9617.3	9707.4	10738.6	11314.9
Finance, Insurance and Real Estate	4846.1	5174.7	5541.3	5943.4	6336.9	6759.8	7309.2
Transportation, Communication and Public Utilities	4575.7	5179.2	5278.0	5383.5	5582.6	5861.3	6287.0
Services	4875.1	5242.9	5323.8	5452.9	5496.3	5995.1	6483.6
Government	6421.9	6879.8	7267.9	7372.9	7540.0	7822.4	8225.2
Farm	4196.3	4046.0	4226.9	4815.2	4486.6	5442.4	5068.5
Total	52435.9	56144.8	57984.9	60500.0	59474.4	66704.2	69181.6

Economic Sector	1957	1958	1959	1960	1961	1962	1963
Mining	2638.1	2313.8	2471.6	2472.3	2427.6	2487.3	2615.5
Construction	3404.0	3347.1	3541.0	3418.8	3279.1	3391.5	3532.8
Manufacturing	18562.4	17532.7	19567.0	20006.3	20398.7	22938.2	24371.0
Trade	11542.9	11526.8	12400.6	12585.7	12728.7	13753.4	14579.8
Finance, Insurance and Real Estate	7748.6	7949.0	8476.0	8874.8	9244.4	9970.6	10542.7
Transportation, Communication and Public Utilities	6506.1	6407.4	6879.9	7144.0	7325.5	7832.3	8345.5
Services	6799.9	6950.9	7225.2	7455.0	7656.5	8066.9	8404.9
Government	8599.2	8869.9	9087.3	9374.7	9771.7	10132.4	10466.2
Farm	4245.4	4449.3	4971.6	4979.4	5471.7	5236.5	5718.8
Total	70046.6	69346.9	74620.2	76311.0	78303.9	83809.1	88577.2

Economic Sector	1964	1965	1966	1967	1968	1969	1970
Mining	2745.9	2874.5	3067.3	3303.0	3279.9	3510.2	3640.2
Construction	3767.7	4157.0	4497.6	4259.3	4372.0	4449.0	4332.1
Manufacturing	26466.5	29216.1	32357.4	32481.8	36518.9	36397.7	40173.9
Trade	15672.0	17033.6	18310.6	18930.3	20124.2	21207.5	21907.6
Finance, Insurance and Real Estate	11272.1	12228.8	12980.1	13535.7	14093.4	14676.9	14450.3
Transportation Communication and Public Utilities	9041.4	9674.4	10655.3	11193.4	12168.2	12908.2	13481.2
Services	8969.1	9536.2	9536.6	9914.2	10347.5	11237.5	11562.7
Government	10816.5	11503.0	12415.9	13130.4	13699.5	14180.8	14720.3
Farm	5955.8	5488.5	5052.6	5563.4	5419.0	5664.5	5639.5
Total	94707.0	101712.1	111801.4	112311.5	120022.6	124232.3	129907.8

APPENDIX TABLE III

GROSS STATE PRODUCT, VIRGINIA, 1950-70

(Millions of Dollars)

Economic Sector	1950	1951	1952	1953	1954	1955	1956
Mining	130.9	147.2	148.2	123.2	99.8	127.4	157.9
Construction	213.7	264.5	292.9	290.1	271.1	302.1	351.2
Manufacturing	1286.3	1490.8	1485.2	1553.7	1510.1	1762.2	1820.6
Trade	795.1	895.6	974.7	993.9	1016.8	1105.1	1188.3
Finance, Insurance and Real Estate	435.8	495.1	582.8	636.1	699.1	784.8	843.0
Transportation, Communication and Public Utilities	486.2	572.8	609.1	626.0	634.1	699.3	782.1
Services	390.0	450.0	477.2	501.2	512.4	582.5	659.8
Government	983.4	1360.3	1534.4	1572.7	1508.2	1541.9	1601.6
Farm	373.5	442.5	422.4	335.8	369.4	351.0	370.0
Total	5094.9	6118.8	6526.9	6632.7	6621.0	7256.3	7774.5

Economic Sector	1957	1958	1959	1960	1961	1962	1963
Mining	167.3	149.5	156.4	154.9	155.0	158.2	167.6
Construction	370.3	364.9	395.2	403.2	449.0	507.4	583.4
Manufacturing	1942.9	1890.0	2072.4	2121.5	2172.2	2413.3	2467.8
Trade	1223.7	1233.9	1355.2	1399.5	1467.6	1598.3	1702.2
Finance, Insurance and Real Estate	876.1	914.6	989.8	1047.7	1118.2	1215.8	1360.6
Transportation Communication and Public Utilities	834.6	830.8	880.9	923.2	948.7	1007.6	1065.2
Services	718.4	747.2	821.1	902.5	959.5	1056.4	1168.0
Government	1693.9	1754.4	1843.1	1915.7	2031.3	2242.8	2451.8
Farm	282.9	382.6	324.6	349.5	370.4	372.1	287.4
Total	8110.1	8267.9	8838.7	9217.7	9671.9	10571.9	11254.0

Economic Sector	1964	1965	1966	1967	1968	1969	1970
Mining	165.6	174.1	179.0	180.8	196.1	221.7	267.1
Construction	638.6	698.5	753.6	753.1	822.6	907.1	990.0
Manufacturing	2696.2	2907.5	3210.2	3297.9	3822.5	3804.4	4252.7
Trade	1870.6	2016.6	2203.8	2358.7	2607.8	2885.0	3123.7
Finance, Insurance and Real Estate	1473.1	1615.7	1740.8	1848.4	1989.0	2185.1	2362.9
Transportation, Communication and Public Utilities	1158.6	1228.8	1324.1	1396.2	1515.6	1601.2	1721.5
Services	1300.2	1415.7	1461.2	1615.4	1773.0	2031.5	2260.4
Government	2755.0	2968.0	3342.0	3828.5	4261.0	4676.2	5148.0
Farm	372.4	365.6	329.4	382.6	364.6	409.4	426.4
Total	12430.3	13390.5	14544.1	15661.6	17352.2	18721.6	20552.7

APPENDIX TABLE IV

GROSS STATE PRODUCT, WEST VIRGINIA, 1950-70

(Millions of Dollars)

Economic Sector	1950	1951	1952	1953	1954	1955	1956
Mining	828.7	938.7	881.5	766.3	640.9	763.8	889.7
Construction	87.1	93.0	102.2	122.6	100.5	108.6	134.0
Manufacturing	818.1	947.7	934.5	1014.0	893.4	1009.8	1071.7
Trade	361.3	396.4	407.1	409.5	400.4	432.5	472.9
Finance, Insurance and Real Estate	147.8	163.7	180.8	199.7	204.3	216.9	242.0
Transportation, Communication and Public Utilities	306.0	350.2	361.4	370.9	347.2	381.5	422.8
Services	176.1	190.0	195.0	209.7	207.6	227.5	250.6
Government	148.5	169.0	182.6	178.3	184.2	191.1	211.3
Farm	109.0	130.9	125.1	101.8	111.8	91.7	90.4
Total	2982.6	3379.6	3370.2	3372.8	3090.3	3423.3	3785.4

Economic Sector	1957	1958	1959	1960	1961	1962	1963
Mining	918.9	713.6	694.3	678.6	624.3	632.6	655.6
Construction	194.4	138.6	134.5	126.7	134.1	134.8	141.8
Manufacturing	1084.6	1061.8	1222.3	1227.4	1209.2	1455.5	1608.1
Trade	504.8	494.1	507.7	506.3	505.3	518.5	540.2
Finance, Insurance and Real Estate	268.4	278.4	283.4	294.8	294.9	307.0	318.2
Transportation, Communication and Public Utilities	444.4	428.9	445.9	450.5	451.7	475.9	496.5
Services	271.0	273.2	289.9	291.8	300.0	315.5	338.2
Government	240.2	259.1	276.7	276.9	309.0	319.2	351.8
Farm	77.4	90.3	82.1	84.7	78.4	70.3	66.7
Total	4004.1	3738.0	3936.8	3937.7	3906.9	4229.3	4517.1

Economic Sector	1964	1965	1966	1967	1968	1969	1970
Mining	675.3	735.0	747.7	757.6	736.1	825.5	982.3
Construction	161.5	185.8	229.1	253.5	275.4	308.7	356.1
Manufacturing	1567.1	1705.5	1840.1	1846.0	1905.7	1780.3	1938.0
Trade	572.4	608.2	671.8	716.8	781.0	824.7	886.6
Finance, Insurance and Real Estate	337.6	362.4	386.0	400.9	420.8	446.9	476.4
Transportation, Communication and Public Utilities	520.2	546.7	582.9	592.7	624.7	635.8	670.3
Services	379.7	415.1	423.8	468.7	499.9	550.5	610.2
Government	378.9	406.6	445.5	485.6	527.2	571.7	643.2
Farm	66.6	66.2	57.8	71.7	64.1	74.0	70.9
Total	4659.3	5031.5	5384.7	5593.5 ·	5834.9	6018.1	6634.0

APPENDIX TABLE V

GROSS STATE PRODUCT, NORTH CAROLINA, 1950-70

(Millions of Dollars)

Economic Sector	1950	1951	1952	1953	1954	1955	1956
Mining	18.9	20.2	23.1	23.2	26.9	28.4	31.5
Construction	216.0	255.5	255.4	244.0	236.7	274.6	296.9
Manufacturing	1787.9	1993.9	2001.2	2156.7	2032.3	2426.3	2517.9
Trade	815.2	898.7	971.9	985.6	998.7	1105.1	1196.8
Finance, Insurance and Real Estate	338.5	387.4	446.1	509.6	555.9	615.3	590.9
Transportation, Communication and Public Utilities	317.9	368.8	408.9	435.5	441.7	484.5	525.0
Services	407.8	445.3	465.3	494.1	512.4	577.8	642.8
Government	478.0	579.8	652.2	668.7	702.8	731.6	736.2
Farm	730.4	880.0	788.3	771.7	762.5	794.4	783.2
Total	5110.6	5829.6	6012.4	6289.1	6269.9	7038.0	7321.2

Economic Sector	1957	1958	1959	1960	1961	1962	1963
Mining	28.8	25.9	26.1	31.4	40.9	41.2	32.7
Construction	287.0	284.5	330.3	337.1	355.7	377.3	411.0
Manufacturing	2640.6	2732.4	3090.1	3277.0	3382.0	3756.9	3814.8
Trade	1218.1	1214.1	1349.3	1395.1	1463.2	1593.9	1696.3
Finance, Insurance and Real Estate	630.1	771.4	850.0	928.9	1019.9	1110.6	1201.5
Transportation, Communication and Public Utilities	548.2	565.2	624.3	644.3	683.3	755.2	796.6
Services	681.2	711.6	771.1	818.3	871.2	933.2	1007.4
Government	812.7	874.0	924.3	981.7	1106.5	1217.6	1291.1
Farm	602.7	735.7	688.0	788.0	831.8	845.8	857.9
Total	7449.4	7914.8	8653.5	9201.8	9754.5	10631.7	11109.3

Economic Sector	1964	1965	1966	1967	1968	1969	1970
Mining	31.9	36.6	39.9	46.2	50.6	51.5	53.9
Construction	453.4	536.3	652.3	676.9	726.4	842.6	878.3
Manufacturing	4144.5	4652.7	5197.7	5415.9	6469.5	6624.7	7834.9
Trade	1852.5	2015.0	2280.1	2476.4	2754.4	3021.4	3284.7
Finance, Insurance and Real Estate	1304.1	1441.0	1573.8	1717.6	1874.8	2067.4	2241.7
Transportation, Communication and Public Utilities	884.8	970.4	1067.3	1139.2	1274.8	1382.6	1463.8
Services	1102.4	1197.0	1270.3	1415.8	1544.1	1772.6	1973.4
Government	1396.1	1509.2	1720.3	1985.9	2234.9	2405.7	2618.1
Farm	876.4	760.6	874.7	886.2	830.6	1013.8	1042.4
Total	12046.1	13118.8	14676.4	15760.1	17760.1	19182.3	21391.2

APPENDIX TABLE VI

GROSS STATE PRODUCT, SOUTH CAROLINA, 1950-70

(Millions of Dollars)

Economic Sector	1950	1951	1952	1953	1954	1955	1956
Mining	9.6	11.0	11.6	10.7	11.5	12.1	13.8
Construction	83.6	155.5	328.2	328.4	201.3	137.3	138.7
Manufacturing	829.7	923.8	901.3	976.9	886.3	1237.6	1288.2
Trade	347.2	390.8	431.1	433.1	429.4	474.8	495.4
Finance, Insurance and Real Estate	155.7	183.8	217.0	248.8	265.7	291.8	326.8
Transportation, Communication and Public Utilities	137.8	158.1	169.7	178.6	177.0	191.6	204.3
Services	177.3	194.8	204.5	216.6	220.7	250.0	283.9
Government	235.8	409.8	440.1	425.1	435.0	433.3	456.7
Farm	256.4	366.7	305.2	294.9	210.5	280.6	232.2
Total	2233.1	2794.3	3008.7	3113.1	2837.4	3309.1	3440.1

Economic Sector	1957	1958	1959	1960	1961	1962	1963
Mining	11.5	11.9	14.0	14.6	15.1	16.2	17.4
Construction	140.9	150.4	158.8	174.3	171.4	190.4	194.9
Manufacturing	1222.5	1149.3	1356.5	1472.5	1480.3	1721.0	1767.3
Trade	510.5	512.6	553.9	571.3	588.5	642.9	683.0
Finance, Insurance and Real Estate	367.0	338.0	379.1	413.3	430.1	467.0	493.9
Transportation, Communication and Public Utilities	217.8	227.8	242.0	247.4	259.8	283.3	303.8
Services	310.6	319.5	350.9	383.3	399.3	428.7	475.6
Government	498.5	520.3	565.4	600.6	621.2	667.8	713.5
Farm	209.2	219.2	233.1	236.2	267.4	262.7	272.0
Total	3488.5	3449.0	3853.7	4113.5	4233.1	4680.0	4921.4

Economic Sector	1964	1965	1966	1967	1968	1969	1970
Mining	17.0	19.3	19.0	20.2	20.2	21.7	23.1
Construction	211.3	265.8	332.8	350.6	382.4	403.4	434.4
Manufacturing	2001.8	2316.3	2525.7	2511.5	2888.2	2883.4	3281.1
Trade	744.1	810.7	919.7	1002.5	1119.2	1254.4	1350.8
Finance, Insurance and Real Estate	536.1	614.0	677.4	738.6	804.6	877.3	933.0
Transportation, Communication and Public Utilities	333.1	354.7	399.3	421.8	472.0	538.1	584.5
Services	540.7	580.4	612.4	687.2	758.1	889.2	979.4
Government	757.7	841.7	1007.0	1129.9	1255.5	1372.2	1488.4
Farm	263.5	261.2	250.9	256.3	220.9	259.9	265.8
Total	5405.3	6064.1	6744.2	7118.6	7921.1	8499.6	9340.5

Appendix Tables

APPENDIX TABLE VII

GROSS STATE PRODUCT, GEORGIA, 1950-70

(Millions of Dollars)

Economic Sector	1950	1951	1952	1953	1954	1955	1956
Mining	24.7	27.7	30.8	28.6	32.6	38.5	45.4
Construction	185.5	216.9	311.1	250.8	238.0	263.2	293.5
Manufacturing	1181.7	1417.6	1402.6	1509.9	1506.7	1907.5	2002.8
Trade	827.9	936.8	1001.5	1024.4	1044.5	1149.0	1259.0
Finance, Insurance and Real Estate	424.1	495.3	562.6	632.0	674.5	737.4	835.4
Transportation, Communication and Public Utilities	406.9	464.1	498.9	525.6	527.6	582.1	628.9
Services	310.2	457.2	490.0	511.7	525.5	597.8	675.1
Government	447.5	635.8	740.8	739.4	772.6	800.7	833.3
Farm	421.4	527.3	459.6	488.0	338.2	418.9	365.1
Total	4229.9	5178.7	5497.9	5710.4	5660.2	6495.1	6938.5

Economic Sector	1957	1958	1959	1960	1961	1962	1963
Mining	46.1	45.8	54.2	54.5	58.1	50.3	61.0
Construction	282.9	302.4	328.0	326.6	313.7	360.8	392.1
Manufacturing	2007.9	1876.4	2168.1	2239.8	2187.6	2587.3	2807.7
Trade	1297.4	1311.5	1442.0	1487.4	1531.8	1667.9	1790.0
Finance, Insurance and Real Estate	876.2	926.5	1021.7	1109.0	1179.6	1257.8	1368.9
Transportation, Communication and Public Utilities	667.7	690.8	759.0	801.2	849.0	922.8	989.3
Services	702.8	719.9	773.4	817.1	857.8	917.4	985.4
Government	894.1	933.1	1002.1	1063.2	1132.6	1265.7	1386.4
Farm	332.0	417.9	411.4	433.6	450.5	426.7	524.8
Total	7107.1	7224.3	7959.9	8332.4	8560.7	9456.7	10305.6

Economic Sector	1964	1965	1966	1967	1968	1969	1970
Mining	63.7	68.8	73.7	80.8	91.0	97.0	105.8
Construction	443.9	523.3	567.9	628.3	702.4	793.5	789.4
Manufacturing	3107.2	3529.1	3988.4	3937.6	4488.0	4552.5	4656.6
Trade	2001.6	2197.7	2405.5	2610.0	2911.8	3336.5	3646.1
Finance, Insurance and Real Estate	1519.5	1696.8	1831.0	1975.0	2144.3	2404.4	2690.0
Transportation, Communication and Public Utilities	1085.8	1179.8	1316.3	1419.7	1574.4	1721.6	1857.7
Services	1102.3	1211.9	1277.4	1401.5	1520.7	1798.1	1987.8
Government	1546.1	1642.9	1912.2	2172.8	2394.7	2603.0	2766.0
Farm	484.1	533.1	550.2	569.5	538.9	672.5	632.9
Total	11354.2	12583.4	13922.6	14795.2	16366.2	17979.1	19132.3

APPENDIX TABLE VIII

GROSS STATE PRODUCT, FLORIDA, 1950-70

(Millions of Dollars)

Economic Sector	1950	1951	1952	1953	1954	1955	1956
Mining	39.9	46.0	55.9	57.2	65.2	66.7	76.9
Construction	287.2	333.9	366.8	420.6	417.5	504.6	614.8
Manufacturing	489.8	609.4	649.8	773.0	813.4	1081.2	1172.3
Trade	920.4	1039.7	1169.2	1216.0	1263.3	1437.3	1630.2
Finance, Insurance and Real Estate	649.8	718.9	795.7	929.6	1017.9	1171.2	1377.8
Transportation, Communication and Public Utilities	416.5	479.3	536.2	581.8	623.8	701.0	785.7
Services	550.8	622.2	689.7	774.0	824.3	948.1	1123.7
Government	469.6	612.5	767.2	838.6	865.8	927.0	1016.9
Farm	376.6	396.1	373.6	395.2	402.0	476.1	493.1
Total	4200.6	4858.0	5404.1	5986.0	6293.2	7313.2	8291.4

Economic Sector	1957	1958	1959	1960	1961	1962	1963
Mining	80.7	83.6	88.2	102.6	92.6	97.5	106.8
Construction	699.7	756.7	814.7	801.9	687.0	716.7	791.2
Manufacturing	1273.1	1317.0	1540.9	1699.5	1825.8	2036.0	2112.2
Trade	1790.9	1939.7	2134.8	2218.9	2264.8	2490.1	2624.8
Finance, Insurance and Real Estate	1582.7	1705.8	1947.6	2091.3	2178.9	2389.5	2515.9
Transportation, Communication and Public Utilities	866.3	920.4	1037.4	1118.7	1163.3	1231.0	1308.6
Services	1279.7	1373.4	1494.3	1586.2	1652.7	1827.6	1997.8
Government	1103.2	1229.8	1302.6	1377.0	1515.6	1625.3	1810.6
Farm	472.1	500.7	604.8	547.0	618.6	643.2	646.5
Total	9148.4	9827.1	10965.3	11543.1	11999.3	13056.9	13914.4

Economic Sector	1964	1965	1966	1967	1968	1969	1970
Mining	121.1	139.6	139.0	121.2	127.4	124.7	136.5
Construction	916.4	1047.8	1098.5	1125.7	1289.4	1691.1	1933.6
Manufacturing	2298.6	2446.5	2702.1	3061.5	3507.6	3665.3	4104.5
Trade	2900.7	3172.8	3544.0	3861.3	4367.7	5004.8	5637.0
Finance, Insurance and Real Estate	2667.5	2945.9	3228.8	3494.1	3827.0	4402.6	4911.3
Transportation, Communication and Public Utilities	1458.2	1562.0	1751.2	1935.2	2187.4	2487.9	2739.1
Services	2198.5	2405.2	2555.9	2857.9	3131.4	3740.0	4197.2
Government	2011.5	2174.5	2395.6	2768.1	3089.3	3448.0	3914.5
Farm	728.2	695.8	714.0	772.7	852.4	935.4	849.6
Total	15300.7	16590.1	18129.1	19997.7	22379.6	25499.8	28423.3

Appendix Tables

APPENDIX TABLE IX

GROSS STATE PRODUCT, KENTUCKY, 1950-70

(Millions of Dollars)

Economic Sector	1950	1951	1952	1953	1954	1955	1956
Mining	379.2	392.0	369.5	335.8	303.3	339.9	386.6
Construction	146.9	237.4	382.7	365.5	287.2	247.2	254.3
Manufacturing	1039.9	1229.3	1207.8	1363.2	1249.5	1681.8	1711.8
Trade	561.7	622.1	786.8	698.2	707.8	778.7	818.6
Finance, Insurance and Real Estate	241.1	267.6	301.4	338.4	367.9	394.4	425.6
Transportation, Communication and Public Utilities	372.4	421.5	493.5	454.2	448.6	473.8	523.3
Services	264.8	287.3	305.5	331.4	341.6	385.6	416.7
Government	322.2	462.6	519.2	511.6	492.2	514.0	485.5
Farm	420.9	525.1	487.6	453.4	474.6	417.8	456.3
Total	3749.1	4444.9	4854.0	4851.7	4672.7	5233.2	5478.7

Economic Sector	1957	1958	1959	1960	1961	1962	1963
Mining	388.3	348.8	340.4	351.9	331.3	333.7	348.4
Construction	251.6	242.5	281.6	270.8	287.0	352.5	375.5
Manufacturing	1831.9	1686.0	1919.6	1834.8	1850.8	2057.3	2332.1
Trade	873.6	890.4	953.1	958.0	965.2	1038.4	1095.2
Finance, Insurance and Real Estate	481.6	532.8	546.8	581.1	598.0	652.1	699.1
Transportation, Communication and Public Utilities	555.2	538.3	564.1	577.9	593.0	641.5	689.4
Services	461.8	484.8	521.5	541.9	571.0	621.4	667.9
Government	529.6	575.1	604.3	654.9	724.6	806.6	819.8
Farm	397.7	453.9	444.6	441.6	505.5	517.7	547.6
Total	5771.3	5752.6	6176.0	6212.9	6426.4	7021.2	7575.0

Economic Sector	1964	1965	1966	1967	1968	1969	1970
Mining	342.1	352.5	368.5	381.9	392.3	435.6	530.4
Construction	365.6	410.4	488.4	522.8	589.3	664.2	632.6
Manufacturing	2522.7	2826.0	3152.9	3215.3	3668.1	3802.2	4198.2
Trade	1192.8	1281.5	1415.4	1529.1	1664.8	1798.4	1939.2
Finance, Insurance and Real Estate	768.2	844.1	913.4	983.3	1049.6	1133.1	1203.7
Transportation, Communication and Public Utilities	731.1	770.1	912.4	851.4	924.2	970.9	1030.7
Services	732.5	794.2	818.4	793.7	998.7	1130.1	1258.0
Government	867.2	919.5	1076.4	1235.2	1381.6	1443.6	1551.2
Farm	454.0	544.9	574.1	596.0	595.0	670.1	647.9
Total	7976.2	8743.2	9719.9	10108.7	11263.6	12048.2	12991.9

APPENDIX TABLE X

GROSS STATE PRODUCT, TENNESSEE, 1950-70

(Millions of Dollars)

Economic Sector	1950	1951	1952	1953	1954	1955	1956
Mining	74.0	75.5	71.2	60.6	61.5	72.8	82.9
Construction	205.8	256.7	245.2	298.1	316.9	265.5	270.4
Manufacturing	1291.3	1362.5	1389.4	1571.7	1480.0	1817.5	1866.6
Trade	728.3	807.0	860.7	859.2	881.1	966.7	1050.0
Finance, Insurance and Real Estate	365.8	407.4	438.1	509.6	588.7	556.1	620.6
Transportation, Communication and Public Utilities	360.4	402.8	429.3	449.2	446.8	472.1	510.9
Services	356.9	384.7	413.6	428.6	446.0	515.3	574.9
Government	335.9	412.9	460.1	483.1	493.2	522.5	547.4
Farm	396.1	466.2	431.1	434.6	360.9	408.1	370.2
Total	4114.5	4575.3	4738.7	5094.7	5075.1	5591.6	5893.9

Economic Sector	1957	1958	1959	1960	1961	1962	1963
Mining	71.2	63.7	68.2	69.1	68.8	73.7	74.1
Construction	251.4	241.4	277.0	285.8	314.9	333.6	358.9
Manufacturing	1902.3	1921.3	2186.4	2225.7	2378.3	2633.7	2770.4
Trade	1131.5	1084.9	1188.8	1220.6	1269.0	1362.8	1437.3
Finance, Insurance and Real Estate	678.9	668.1	746.2	818.5	872.3	959.1	1021.5
Transportation, Communication and Public Utilities	527.1	522.2	555.2	570.4	591.0	633.8	675.7
Services	609.2	641.5	690.9	227.0	771.9	826.0	886.1
Government	604.7	662.2	701.6	721.1	773.6	839.4	931.6
Farm	336.5	394.5	406.6	367.8	414.5	387.9	431.6
Total	6112.8	6199.8	6820.9	6506.0	7454.3	8050.0	8587.2

Economic Sector	1964	1965	1966	1967	1968	1969	1970
Mining	76.5	83.8	84.2	84.8	91.0	93.1	101.9
Construction	391.7	445.7	541.5	547.0	589.3	646.3	633.9
Manufacturing	3107.9	3445.5	3883.7	4058.0	4676.3	4749.1	5355.1
Trade	1554.4	1689.0	1897.6	2032.8	2218.0	2428.6	2568.3
Finance, Insurance and Real Estate	1110.1	1227.8	1329.2	1413.7	1539.8	1681.4	1773.1
Transportation, Communication and Real Estate	717.2	766.2	830.1	871.0	951.8	1026.4	1081.1
Services	953.8	1050.3	1114.6	1224.9	1339.7	1519.7	1692.2
Government	1027.1	1121.2	1188.1	1314.5	1441.4	1580.0	1733.3
Farm	402.0	426.9	421.5	395.0	404.7	463.4	489.7
Total	9340.7	10256.4	11290.5	11941.7	13252.0	14188.0	15428.6

APPENDIX TABLE XI

GROSS STATE PRODUCT, ALABAMA, 1950-70

(Millions of Dollars)

Economic Sector	1950	1951	1952	1953	1954	1955	1956
Mining	138.5	136.2	129.0	126.8	111.3	125.5	140.1
Construction	126.6	170.3	202.1	156.3	155.5	180.8	241.5
Manufacturing	1014.7	1210.8	1162.4	1268.7	1205.3	1447.1	1482.7
Trade	566.1	627.8	670.5	667.7	669.1	734.9	803.2
Finance, Insurance and Real Estate	291.5	323.5	361.7	387.4	425.1	465.3	530.9
Transportation, Communication and Public Utilities	290.7	336.5	356.4	376.0	366.0	383.3	415.8
Services	273.0	296.9	313.7	344.3	352.2	399.8	448.6
Government	286.4	429.8	518.2	543.2	519.7	567.1	612.5
Farm	335.0	391.3	375.4	399.7	290.4	425.0	316.8
Total	3322.5	3923.1	4089.4	4270.1	4094.6	4728.8	4992.1

Economic Sector	1957	1958	1959	1960	1961	1962	1963
Mining	148.1	127.6	132.4	148.7	133.3	119.2	106.8
Construction	269.0	241.4	252.6	254.6	246.1	243.6	268.0
Manufacturing	1560.5	1496.4	1615.8	1680.7	1637.2	1811.3	1930.6
Trade	831.0	843.4	931.4	944.9	968.1	1028.0	1080.3
Finance, Insurance and Real Estate	556.4	572.6	642.6	638.4	659.4	706.8	761.9
Transportation, Communication and Public Utilities	439.3	452.1	487.8	509.6	525.2	554.9	588.2
Services	471.4	513.2	556.2	579.3	613.5	640.9	703.5
Government	686.1	742.8	794.5	860.1	913.9	1009.9	1057.6
Farm	271.2	329.2	337.8	335.9	331.8	319.6	390.8
Total	5233.0	5318.7	5751.1	5952.2	6028.5	6434.2	6887.7

Economic Sector	1964	1965	1966	1967	1968	1969	1970
Mining	112.5	116.1	109.4	115.1	117.2	132.7	149.9
Construction	341.8	384.6	440.0	431.3	448.7	497.9	497.3
Manufacturing	2173.2	2455.2	2833.9	2922.3	3319.9	3533.5	3868.9
Trade	1179.2	1263.4	1386.4	1472.3	1594.5	1729.4	1857.6
Finance, Insurance and Real Estate	823.0	903.8	973.4	1055.0	1127.2	1189.9	1252.1
Transportation, Communication and Public Utilities	628.7	665.4	719.4	744.0	806.8	863.7	907.4
Services	790.6	891.2	909.7	985.3	1055.9	1164.0	1271.3
Government	1127.9	1197.9	1325.7	1431.9	1549.0	1695.4	1871.2
Farm	363.9	383.0	344.7	320.4	359.6	440.8	422.0
Total	7540.8	8260.6	9042.6	9477.6	10378.8	11247.3	12097.7

APPENDIX TABLE XII

GROSS STATE PRODUCT, MISSISSIPPI, 1950-70

(Millions of Dollars)

Economic Sector	1950	1951	1952	1953	1954	1955	1956
Mining	22.7	25.8	30.8	30.4	36.4	42.5	49.2
Construction	75.7	97.7	88.5	87.7	80.0	89.7	92.4
Manufacturing	329.1	397.7	413.1	451.4	451.0	566.5	556.8
Trade	342.9	379.4	402.9	395.6	400.4	426.9	455.8
Finance, Insurance and Real Estate	124.5	135.8	148.8	179.4	196.3	205.0	230.3
Transportation, Communication and Public Utilities	136.0	156.4	164.6	174.8	182.2	193.5	211.5
Services	162.0	179.3	189.1	196.3	221.8	230.0	257.6
Government	192.7	240.8	257.5	262.6	285.8	286.7	302.6
Farm	430.0	468.3	522.4	506.7	385.7	493.5	386.8
Total	1815.6	2081.2	2217.7	2284.9	2239.6	2533.8	2543.0

Economic Sector	1957	1958	1959	1960	1961	1962	1963
Mining	59.6	65.8	80.2	85.8	86.2	88.8	95.9
Construction	99.0	123.6	132.1	123.2	136.4	140.8	160.6
Manufacturing	586.6	584.4	667.2	682.5	714.8	805.9	900.3
Trade	449.5	452.9	498.9	509.3	519.9	559.9	587.7
Finance, Insurance and Real Estate	248.6	258.4	295.3	319.2	344.0	366.0	397.6
Transportation, Communication and Real Estate	223.2	224.3	243.9	252.9	263.6	283.3	294.0
Services	273.5	287.5	305.6	325.7	342.5	366.8	388.6
Government	318.4	346.2	380.5	420.3	445.0	485.3	504.2
Farm	315.5	333.3	432.6	395.7	472.5	436.1	581.5
Total	2573.9	2676.4	3036.3	3114.6	3324.9	3532.9	3910.4

Economic Sector	1964	1965	1966	1967	1968	1969	1970
Mining	91.3	88.0	86.3	89.0	97.0	106.9	113.5
Construction	170.9	212.8	247.2	255.9	245.3	286.1	296.7
Manufacturing	986.3	1072.1	1341.3	1389.9	1631.3	1596.5	1896.7
Trade	631.0	685.3	762.1	815.3	885.4	959.6	1021.3
Finance, Insurance and Real Estate	422.1	468.9	518.8	565.5	612.6	649.8	682.5
Transportation, Communication and Public Utilities	315.3	383.2	359.7	376.9	413.2	452.0	470.5
Services	413.2	476.1	488.3	530.7	575.9	644.9	688.6
Government	532.2	576.5	655.8	697.5	810.9	880.1	934.5
Farm	530.4	522.1	450.0	483.1	519.3	515.5	594.5
Total	4092.7	4485.0	4909.5	5203.8	5790.9	6091.4	6698.8

Appendix Tables

APPENDIX TABLE XIII

GROSS STATE PRODUCT, ARKANSAS, 1950-70

(Millions of Dollars)

Economic Sector	1950	1951	1952	1953	1954	1955	1956
Mining	51.2	55.3	59.7	57.2	59.5	66.7	69.1
Construction	81.4	120.4	132.9	106.8	79.0	78.9	78.6
Manufacturing	323.1	391.0	390.7	418.4	435.7	574.7	595.1
Trade	325.8	362.6	381.8	377.6	374.0	404.2	426.3
Finance, Insurance and Real Estate	136.1	143.9	160.8	175.3	188.1	201.1	214.6
Transportation, Communication and Public Utilities	170.0	193.8	203.7	209.2	207.9	221.9	236.1
Services	150.2	161.5	168.0	179.2	181.5	200.4	218.3
Government	128.5	184.8	204.7	220.5	231.8	234.7	251.8
Farm	386.8	466.4	443.6	420.2	379.3	460.8	406.5
Total	1753.1	2079.7	2145.9	2164.4	2136.8	2443.4	2496.4

Economic Sector	1957	1958	1959	1960	1961	1962	1963
Mining	75.0	67.7	66.2	62.9	66.6	60.1	63.2
Construction	101.2	99.9	104.3	117.4	142.4	169.1	180.7
Manufacturing	626.2	533.7	641.1	651.1	692.0	765.8	873.7
Trade	439.5	454.4	491.8	499.2	524.3	574.7	617.4
Finance, Insurance and Real Estate	236.8	262.6	287.4	307.0	327.7	370.2	401.9
Transportation, Communication and Public Utilities	240.7	251.2	276.7	284.3	325.7	348.7	352.5
Services	235.1	254.2	274.6	289.5	309.7	341.2	368.9
Government	290.5	299.9	295.1	295.4	332.9	365.1	391.3
Farm	335.7	357.1	475.4	431.8	500.4	486.3	507.8
Total	2580.7	2580.7	2912.6	2938.6	3221.7	3481.2	3757.4

Economic Sector	1964	1965	1966	1967	1968	1969	1970
Mining	63.7	64.5	69.5	68.8	70.7	75.1	76.9
Construction	180.5	216.4	252.0	262.0	257.4	264.5	249.3
Manufacturing	984.5	1075.3	1281.6	1352.8	1605.3	1715.5	1956.1
Trade	673.2	704.9	749.8	810.7	896.3	962.7	1026.1
Finance, Insurance and Real Estate	443.2	490.4	523.2	565.5	608.6	657.9	698.7
Transportation, Communication and Public Utilities	388.2	406.0	434.8	445.2	479.8	503.7	530.3
Services	404.6	428.8	429.8	482.7	532.6	602.6	661.8
Government	416.1	429.6	473.7	518.2	566.3	619.1	696.1
Farm	577.3	529.2	586.4	495.2	553.8	670.2	578.3
Total	4131.3	4345.1	4800.8	5001.1	5570.8	6071.3	6473.6

APPENDIX TABLE XIV

GROSS STATE PRODUCT, LOUISIANA, 1950-70

(Millions of Dollars)

Economic Sector	1950	1951	1952	1953	1954	1955	1956
Mining	242.8	263.5	313.7	330.5	401.1	501.8	587.9
Construction	193.4	234.0	264.6	300.3	277.7	259.8	321.2
Manufacturing	935.0	1091.4	1110.5	1153.6	1102.8	1306.6	1471.0
Trade	670.0	723.8	766.3	791.2	832.5	907.4	986.6
Finance, Insurance and Real Estate	319.1	355.4	397.9	448.5	494.6	532.4	581.6
Transportation, Communication and Public Utilities	433.5	503.2	551.5	581.8	586.0	637.2	703.0
Services	364.1	383.5	400.7	426.2	443.6	498.8	553.5
Government	308.5	388.6	467.5	489.4	492.2	487.4	565.5
Farm	252.2	338.7	344.9	329.9	272.0	285.9	253.1
Total	3718.6	4282.1	4617.6	4851.4	4902.5	5497.3	6023.4

Economic Sector	1957	1958	1959	1960	1961	1962	1963
Mining	626.7	609.9	632.1	643.0	679.9	706.2	731.7
Construction	415.7	401.1	374.4	347.4	346.4	359.6	395.6
Manufacturing	1482.3	1549.8	1384.2	1394.7	1419.9	1514.4	1668.9
Trade	1076.2	1094.9	1180.1	1177.3	1182.8	1254.6	1325.8
Finance, Insurance and Real Estate	659.0	719.8	774.2	806.3	831.4	866.6	929.3
Transportation, Communication and Public Utilities	766.0	755.4	797.2	827.1	847.1	890.0	944.5
Services	615.3	624.9	676.8	699.3	727.1	776.1	821.2
Government	661.5	673.0	688.6	717.8	774.7	863.5	899.8
Farm	226.9	234.9	279.6	258.6	291.9	287.6	358.0
Total	6529.6	6663.7	6787.2	6871.5	7101.2	7518.6	8074.8

Economic Sector	1964	1965	1966	1967	1968	1969	1970
Mining	771.2	846.8	890.8	929.6	985.0	1076.9	1022.5
Construction	483.0	584.5	768.1	843.0	911.7	855.8	846.3
Manufacturing	1828.1	2013.3	2309.4	2364.4	2699.6	2660.4	2984.0
Trade	1439.8	1571.3	1761.3	1894.6	2084.1	2256.3	2386.3
Finance, Insurance and Real Estate	1012.9	1125.4	1239.2	1321.0	1409.1	1506.8	1583.2
Transportation, Communication and Public Utilities	1036.5	1099.4	1160.2	1257.5	1357.1	1445.8	1503.2
Services	910.5	989.5	1025.6	1142.3	1241.6	1404.7	1533.0
Government	952.7	1043.4	1174.0	1297.2	1439.2	1555.8	1709.0
Farm	334.4	315.4	342.0	316.1	432.0	378.3	439.2
Total	8770.1	9589.0	10670.6	11365.7	12559.4	13140.8	14006.7

APPENDIX TABLE XV

REAL GROSS STATE PRODUCT, VIRGINIA, 1950-70

(Millions of 1958 Dollars)

Economic Sector	1950	1951	1952	1953	1954	1955	1956
Mining	152.3	170.2	171.3	140.6	107.4	133.3	160.1
Construction	273.3	322.2	331.7	329.7	313.0	348.8	383.0
Manufacturing	1620.1	1756.0	1713.0	1783.8	1698.7	1947.2	1924.6
Trade	935.4	974.5	1048.1	1079.2	1094.9	1196.0	1246.9
Finance, Insurance and Real Estate	581.8	628.3	703.0	727.8	780.2	859.6	903.5
Transportation, Communication and Public Utilities	580.2	673.1	679.8	679.0	706.1	756.0	826.7
Services	530.6	582.1	589.1	592.4	584.9	645.1	700.4
Government	1356.4	1458.0	1546.8	1579.0	1585.9	1623.1	1670.1
Farm	349.9	339.9	353.2	328.5	381.8	392.8	415.5
Total	6379.9	6904.3	7136.0	7240.0	7252.9	7901.9	8230.8

Economic Sector	1957	1958	1959	1960	1961	1962	1963
Mining	168.3	149.5	164.3	159.7	160.0	165.5	178.1
Construction	374.8	364.9	390.5	386.2	410.8	442.8	484.6
Manufacturing	1990.7	1890.0	2039.7	2069.7	2115.1	2349.8	2400.6
Trade	1244.8	1233.9	1335.2	1366.7	1409.8	1533.9	1625.8
Finance, Insurance and Real Estate	909.8	914.6	957.3	995.0	1049.0	1136.3	1250.6
Transportation, Communication and Public Utilities	857.8	830.8	876.5	908.7	926.5	983.0	1045.3
Services	736.8	747.2	793.3	845.0	877.1	941.5	1000.9
Government	1714.5	1754.4	1772.2	1807.3	1898.4	1967.4	2043.2
Farm	313.3	382.6	342.6	372.6	395.2	385.4	302.8
Total	8310.8	8267.9	8671.6	8910.9	9242.4	9905.6	10331.9

Economic Sector	1964	1965	1966	1967	1968	1969	1970
Mining	179.6	183.5	195.6	207.8	216.0	238.4	272.8
Construction	505.6	527.6	532.2	481.5	496.4	494.6	501.3
Manufacturing	2602.5	2790.3	3031.3	3028.4	3431.2	3340.2	3688.3
Trade	1764.7	1909.7	2018.1	2069.0	2197.0	2315.4	2380.9
Finance, Insurance and Real Estate	1329.5	1438.7	1513.7	1555.9	1607.9	1677.0	1640.9
Transportation, Communication and Public Utilities	1131.4	1196.5	1299.4	1364.8	1465.8	1510.6	1594.0
Services	1074.5	1138.9	1125.7	1176.5	1225.3	1325.2	1367.5
Government	2087.1	2205.1	2385.4	2567.7	2691.7	2776.8	2855.2
Farm	406.6	370.8	301.8	381.5	344.1	361.6	374.1
Total	11081.5	11761.5	12331.2	12833.1	13675.4	14039.8	14675.0

APPENDIX TABLE XVI

REAL GROSS STATE PRODUCT, WEST VIRGINIA, 1950-70

(Millions of 1958 Dollars)

Economic Sector	1950	1951	1952	1953	1954	1955	1956
Mining	963.6	1085.2	1019.1	874.8	689.9	799.0	902.3
Construction	111.4	113.3	115.7	139.3	116.1	125.4	146.1
Manufacturing	1030.4	1116.3	1077.8	1164.2	1004.9	1115.7	1132.8
Trade	425.1	431.3	437.7	444.6	431.0	468.1	496.2
Finance, Insurance and Real Estate	197.3	207.7	218.1	228.5	228.0	237.6	259.4
Transportation, Communication and Public Utilities	365.2	411.5	403.3	402.3	386.0	412.4	446.9
Services	239.6	245.8	240.7	247.9	237.0	251.9	266.0
Government	239.9	235.4	240.6	240.3	246.9	246.9	251.8
Farm	102.4	101.4	105.9	99.7	115.9	103.3	102.0
Total	3674.9	3947.9	3858.9	3841.6	3456.3	3760.3	4003.5

Economic Sector	1957	1958	1959	1960	1961	1962	1963
Mining	924.4	713.6	729.3	699.6	644.3	661.7	696.7
Construction	196.8	138.6	132.9	121.4	122.7	117.6	117.8
Manufacturing	1111.2	1061.8	1203.0	1197.4	1177.3	1417.1	1564.2
Trade	513.5	494.1	500.2	494.4	485.4	497.6	516.0
Finance, Insurance and Real Estate	278.7	278.4	274.1	280.0	276.6	286.9	292.5
Transportation, Communication and Public Utilities	456.7	428.9	443.7	443.4	441.1	464.3	487.2
Services	277.9	273.2	280.1	273.2	274.2	281.2	289.8
Government	248.1	259.1	263.3	272.0	288.0	287.8	290.5
Farm	85.7	90.3	86.7	90.4	84.0	73.1	70.5
Total	4093.0	3738.0	3913.3	3871.8	3793.6	4087.3	4325.2

Economic Sector	1964	1965	1966	1967	1968	1969	1970
Mining	732.4	774.5	817.2	870.8	810.7	887.6	1003.4
Construction	127.9	140.3	161.8	162.1	166.2	168.3	189.4
Manufacturing	1512.7	1635.5	1737.5	1695.0	1710.7	1563.0	1680.7
Trade	540.0	575.9	615.2	628.8	658.0	661.9	687.3
Finance, Insurance and Real Estate	304.7	322.7	335.7	337.5	340.2	343.0	330.8
Transportation, Communication and Public Utilities	508.0	532.3	572.0	579.4	604.2	599.8	620.6
Services	313.8	334.0	326.5	341.4	345.5	359.1	369.1
Government	302.2	329.2	356.7	371.3	382.6	382.9	386.5
Farm	73.8	67.6	52.7	71.9	60.6	65.3	62.3
Total	4415.5	4712.0	4975.3	5058.2	5078.7	5030.9	5330.1

Appendix Tables

APPENDIX TABLE XVII

REAL GROSS STATE PRODUCT, NORTH CAROLINA, 1950-70

(Millions of 1958 Dollars)

Economic Sector	1950	1951	1952	1953	1954	1955	1956
Mining	22.0	23.4	26.7	26.5	29.0	29.7	31.9
Construction	276.2	311.2	289.2	277.3	273.3	317.1	323.8
Manufacturing	2251.7	2348.4	2308.1	2476.1	2286.0	2680.9	2661.5
Trade	959.1	977.9	1045.1	1070.1	1075.0	1196.0	1255.8
Finance, Insurance and Real Estate	451.9	491.6	538.1	583.1	620.4	673.9	633.3
Transportation, Communication and Public Utilities	379.4	433.4	456.4	472.3	491.9	523.8	555.0
Services	554.8	576.1	574.4	584.0	584.9	639.9	682.4
Government	633.1	655.1	697.5	707.6	742.9	779.1	861.7
Farm	685.5	684.1	657.4	753.6	782.4	877.5	872.5
Total	6213.7	6501.2	6592.9	6950.6	6885.8	7717.9	7837.9

Economic Sector	1957	1958	1959	1960	1961	1962	1963
Mining	29.0	25.9	27.4	32.4	42.2	43.1	34.8
Construction	290.5	284.5	326.4	322.9	325.4	329.2	341.4
Manufacturing	2705.5	2732.4	3041.3	3197.0	3292.9	3658.0	3710.9
Trade	1239.2	1214.1	1329.4	1362.4	1405.6	1529.7	1620.2
Finance, Insurance and Real Estate	654.3	771.4	822.1	882.1	956.8	1037.9	1104.3
Transportation, Communication and Public Utilities	563.4	565.2	621.2	634.2	667.3	736.8	781.7
Services	698.7	711.6	745.0	766.2	796.3	831.7	863.2
Government	855.5	874.0	897.4	931.4	969.8	1013.8	1053.1
Farm	660.3	735.7	722.4	835.4	883.6	873.0	891.2
Total	7696.4	7914.8	8532.6	8964.0	9339.9	10053.2	10400.8

Economic Sector	1964	1965	1966	1967	1968	1969	1970
Mining	34.6	38.6	43.6	53.1	55.7	55.4	55.1
Construction	359.0	405.1	460.7	432.8	438.1	459.4	444.7
Manufacturing	4000.4	4465.1	4908.1	4973.2	5807.5	5816.2	6795.1
Trade	1747.6	1908.1	2088.0	2172.3	2320.5	2424.9	2503.6
Finance, Insurance and Real Estate	1177.0	1283.2	1368.5	1445.8	1515.6	1586.6	1556.7
Transportation, Communication and Public Utilities	864.1	947.7	1047.4	1113.6	1232.9	1304.3	1355.4
Services	911.1	963.0	978.7	1031.2	1067.1	1156.3	1193.8
Government	1078.9	1143.3	1233.2	1313.4	1386.4	1442.3	1498.6
Farm	949.4	769.3	804.6	881.1	783.2	899.4	916.0
Total	11122.1	11923.4	12932.8	13416.5	14607.0	15144.8	16319.0

APPENDIX TABLE XVIII

REAL GROSS STATE PRODUCT, SOUTH CAROLINA, 1950-70

(Millions of 1958 Dollars)

Economic Sector	1950	1951	1952	1953	1954	1955	1956
Mining	11.2	12.7	13.4	12.2	12.4	12.7	14.0
Construction	106.9	189.4	371.7	373.2	232.4	158.5	151.3
Manufacturing	1044.4	1088.1	1039.0	1121.6	996.9	1367.5	1361.7
Trade	408.5	425.2	463.5	476.2	462.2	513.9	519.8
Finance, Insurance and Real Estate	207.9	233.2	261.8	284.7	296.5	319.6	350.3
Transportation, Communication and Public Utilities	164.4	185.8	189.4	193.7	197.1	207.1	216.0
Service	241.2	252.0	252.5	256.0	280.6	276.9	301.4
Government	364.5	412.3	442.8	441.4	449.8	467.4	484.8
Farm	237.8	281.8	251.7	288.0	217.1	311.7	262.2
Total	2786.8	3080.5	3285.8	3447.0	3145.0	3635.3	3661.5

Economic Sector	1957	1958	1959	1960	1961	1962	1963
Mining	11.6	11.9	15.1	15.1	15.6	17.0	18.5
Construction	142.6	150.4	156.9	167.0	156.8	166.1	161.5
Manufacturing	1252.5	1149.3	1351.4	1436.5	1441.4	1675.7	1719.2
Trade	519.3	512.6	545.7	557.9	565.3	617.0	652.3
Finance, Insurance and Real Estate	381.1	338.0	366.6	392.5	403.5	436.4	454.0
Transportation, Communication and Public Utilities	223.8	227.8	240.8	243.5	253.7	276.4	298.1
Services	318.6	319.5	339.0	358.9	365.0	382.1	407.5
Government	512.3	520.3	530.4	545.0	557.6	564.5	584.8
Farm	230.3	219.2	245.3	252.2	285.5	271.9	283.5
Total	3592.1	3449.0	3791.2	3968.6	4044.4	4407.1	4579.8

Economic Sector	1964	1965	1966	1967	1968	1969	1970
Mining	18.4	20.3	20.8	23.2	22.2	23.3	23.6
Construction	167.3	200.8	235.0	224.2	230.8	220.0	220.0
Manufacturing	1932.1	2222.9	2385.0	2306.2	2592.5	2531.4	2845.7
Trade	702.0	767.7	842.2	879.4	942.9	1006.7	1029.6
Finance, Insurance and Real Estate	483.8	546.7	589.0	621.7	650.4	673.3	647.9
Transportation, Communication and Public Utilities	325.3	345.4	391.9	412.3	456.5	507.6	541.2
Services	466.9	466.9	471.8	500.5	523.9	580.0	592.5
Government	606.9	630.5	686.4	728.5	760.9	798.7	850.5
Farm	288.0	264.8	228.9	255.5	207.4	227.1	231.3
Total	4990.7	5466.0	5851.0	5951.5	6387.5	6568.1	6982.3

Appendix Tables

APPENDIX TABLE XIX

REAL GROSS STATE PRODUCT, GEORGIA, 1950-70

(Millions of 1958 Dollars)

Economic Sector	1950	1951	1952	1953	1954	1955	1956
Mining	28.7	32.0	35.6	32.6	35.1	40.3	46.0
Construction	237.2	264.2	352.3	284.0	274.8	303.9	320.1
Manufacturing	1488.3	1669.7	1617.8	1733.5	1694.8	2107.7	2117.1
Trade	974.0	1019.4	1076.9	1112.3	1124.3	1243.5	1321.1
Finance, Insurance and Real Estate	566.2	628.6	678.6	723.1	752.8	807.7	895.4
Transportation, Communication and Public Utilities	485.6	545.4	556.8	570.1	587.5	629.3	664.8
Services	422.0	591.5	604.9	604.8	599.9	662.0	716.7
Government	641.1	733.3	781.4	784.1	770.3	795.1	838.3
Farm	390.1	397.0	375.1	473.2	349.8	467.4	413.0
Total	5233.2	5881.1	6079.4	6317.7	6189.3	7056.9	7332.5

Economic Sector	1957	1958	1959	1960	1961	1962	1963
Mining	46.4	45.8	56.9	56.2	60.0	52.6	64.8
Construction	286.3	302.1	324.1	312.8	287.0	314.8	325.7
Manufacturing	2057.3	1876.4	2134.0	2185.2	2130.1	2519.2	2731.2
Trade	1319.8	1311.5	1420.7	1452.5	1471.5	1600.7	1790.6
Finance, Insurance and Real Estate	909.0	926.5	988.1	1053.2	1106.6	1175.5	1258.2
Transportation, Communication and Public Utilities	682.2	690.8	755.2	788.6	829.1	900.3	970.9
Services	720.8	719.9	698.9	765.1	784.1	817.6	844.4
Government	892.3	933.1	957.1	989.0	1019.4	1047.8	1084.1
Farm	370.2	417.9	445.6	472.9	485.4	445.7	563.3
Total	7289.2	7224.0	7780.6	8075.5	8173.2	8874.2	9633.2

Economic Sector	1964	1965	1966	1967	1968	1969	1970
Mining	69.1	75.5	80.0	90.1	104.2	106.5	108.1
Construction	351.5	389.1	399.1	409.0	426.8	431.7	399.7
Manufacturing	2999.2	3386.9	3766.2	3615.8	4028.8	4075.6	4038.6
Trade	1888.3	2053.9	2200.8	2289.5	2455.1	2648.0	2779.0
Finance, Insurance and Real Estate	1436.4	1508.3	1585.3	1663.9	1754.7	1785.0	1868.1
Transportation, Communication and Public Utilities	1060.4	1148.8	1291.8	1387.8	1522.6	1624.2	1720.1
Services	911.0	973.4	977.4	1025.2	1051.7	1159.3	1202.5
Government	1120.4	1183.6	1289.4	1376.0	1431.4	1516.0	1582.4
Farm	546.9	551.7	513.4	586.5	516.7	585.7	525.5
Total	10383.2	11271.2	12103.4	12443.1	13291.4	13932.0	14224.0

APPENDIX TABLE XX

REAL GROSS STATE PRODUCT, FLORIDA, 1950-70

(Millions of 1958 Dollars)

Economic Sector	1950	1951	1952	1953	1954	1955	1956
Mining	46.4	53.2	64.6	65.3	70.2	69.8	78.0
Construction	367.3	406.7	415.4	478.0	482.1	582.7	670.4
Manufacturing	616.8	717.8	749.5	887.5	914.9	1194.5	1239.1
Trade	1082.8	1131.3	1257.2	1320.3	1359.8	1555.5	1710.6
Finance, Insurance and Real Estate	867.6	912.3	959.8	1063.6	1136.0	1282.8	1476.7
Transportation, Communication and Public Utilities	497.0	563.2	598.4	631.0	694.7	757.8	830.5
Services	749.4	804.9	851.5	914.4	941.0	1049.9	1192.9
Government	751.4	784.3	857.2	869.9	914.3	991.4	1085.3
Farm	354.4	303.5	311.2	387.7	414.7	528.9	551.4
Total	5333.1	5677.2	6064.8	6618.2	6927.7	8013.3	8834.9

Economic Sector	1957	1958	1959	1960	1961	1962	1963
Mining	81.2	83.6	92.6	105.8	95.6	102.0	113.5
Construction	708.2	756.7	805.0	768.1	628.5	625.4	657.1
Manufacturing	1304.4	1317.0	1516.6	1657.9	1777.8	1982.4	2054.6
Trade	1821.9	1939.7	2103.3	2166.9	2175.6	2390.7	2507.0
Finance, Insurance and Real Estate	1643.5	1705.8	1883.6	1986.0	2044.0	2233.2	2312.4
Transportation, Communication and Public Utilities	890.3	920.4	1032.2	1101.1	1136.0	1201.0	1284.2
Services	1312.5	1373.4	1443.8	1485.2	1510.7	1628.9	1711.9
Government	1169.9	1229.8	1307.8	1389.5	1462.9	1558.3	1635.5
Farm	515.7	500.7	632.0	579.6	656.3	663.3	671.3
Total	9447.6	9827.1	10816.9	11240.1	11487.4	12385.2	12947.5

Economic Sector	1964	1965	1966	1967	1968	1969	1970
Mining	131.3	147.1	151.4	139.3	140.3	134.1	139.4
Construction	725.6	791.4	775.8	719.8	778.2	922.1	979.0
Manufacturing	2218.7	2347.9	2551.5	2811.2	3148.7	3218.0	3559.8
Trade	2736.5	3004.5	3245.4	3387.1	3679.6	4016.7	4296.5
Finance, Insurance and Real Estate	2407.5	2623.2	2807.7	2941.2	3093.8	3378.8	3410.6
Transportation, Communication and Public Utilities	1424.6	1520.9	1718.5	1891.7	2115.5	2397.1	2536.2
Services	1816.9	1935.0	1969.1	2081.5	2164.1	2439.7	2539.1
Government	1731.1	1897.5	2054.5	2155.8	2279.9	2381.2	2506.1
Farm	786.6	703.1	657.4	765.5	804.7	830.2	745.3
Total	13978.2	14970.6	15931.8	16893.1	18204.8	19717.9	20712.0

Appendix Tables

APPENDIX TABLE XXI

REAL GROSS STATE PRODUCT, KENTUCKY, 1950-70

(Millions of 1958 Dollars)

Economic Sector	1950	1951	1952	1953	1954	1955	1956
Mining	440.9	453.2	427.2	383.3	326.5	355.5	392.1
Construction	187.9	289.2	433.4	415.3	331.6	285.5	277.3
Manufacturing	1309.6	1447.9	1393.1	1565.1	1405.5	1858.2	1809.5
Trade	660.8	676.9	846.0	758.1	761.9	842.7	859.0
Finance, Insurance and Real Estate	321.9	339.6	363.6	387.2	410.6	432.0	456.2
Transportation, Communication and Public Utilities	444.4	495.3	490.5	492.6	499.6	512.2	553.2
Services	360.3	371.7	377.2	391.7	390.0	427.0	444.5
Government	445.0	474.9	505.6	512.1	516.5	536.0	558.7
Farm	395.9	410.4	407.0	439.8	484.8	461.0	504.8
Total	4566.7	4959.1	5243.6	5345.2	5127.0	5710.0	5855.3

Economic Sector	1957	1958	1959	1960	1961	1962	1963
Mining	390.6	348.8	357.6	362.8	341.9	349.1	370.2
Construction	254.7	242.5	278.3	259.4	262.6	307.6	311.9
Manufacturing	1831.8	1686.0	1889.2	1790.0	1802.0	2003.2	2268.5
Trade	888.7	890.4	939.0	935.5	927.2	996.5	1046.0
Finance, Insurance and Real Estate	500.1	532.8	528.8	551.9	561.0	609.4	642.6
Transportation, Communication and Public Utilities	570.6	538.3	561.3	568.8	579.1	625.9	676.5
Services	473.6	484.8	503.9	507.4	521.9	553.8	572.3
Government	572.5	575.1	583.9	595.4	619.3	646.3	670.9
Farm	433.3	453.9	466.2	468.7	536.5	532.8	567.3
Total	5915.9	5752.6	6108.2	6039.9	6151.5	6624.6	7126.2

Economic Sector	1964	1965	1966	1967	1968	1969	1970
Mining	371.0	371.4	402.7	439.0	432.0	468.4	541.8
Construction	289.5	310.0	344.9	334.3	355.6	362.2	320.3
Manufacturing	2434.9	2712.0	2977.2	2952.4	3292.6	3338.2	3636.4
Trade	1125.3	1213.5	1296.2	1341.3	1402.5	1443.3	1478.0
Finance, Insurance and Real Estate	693.3	751.6	794.3	827.7	848.5	869.6	835.9
Transportation Communication and Public Utilities	741.0	749.9	895.4	832.3	893.8	915.9	954.4
Services	605.4	638.9	630.5	578.1	690.2	737.2	761.0
Government	689.9	724.6	778.3	833.5	877.8	890.6	925.0
Farm	492.2	548.7	527.2	590.0	563.2	597.4	571.4
Total	7415.5	8020.6	8646.7	8728.6	9356.2	9622.8	10024.2

APPENDIX TABLE XXII

REAL GROSS STATE PRODUCT, TENNESSEE, 1950-70

(Millions of 1958 Dollars)

Economic Sector	1950	1951	1952	1953	1954	1955	1956
Mining	86.0	87.3	82.3	69.2	66.2	76.2	84.1
Construction	263.2	312.7	277.7	338.8	365.9	306.6	294.9
Manufacturing	1626.3	1604.7	1602.4	1804.5	1664.8	2002.8	1973.1
Trade	856.8	878.1	925.5	932.9	948.4	1046.2	1101.8
Finance, Insurance and Real Estate	488.4	517.0	528.5	583.1	657.0	609.1	665.2
Transportation, Communication and Public Utilities	430.1	473.3	479.1	407.2	497.6	510.4	540.1
Services	485.6	497.7	510.6	506.6	509.1	570.7	610.3
Government	514.4	550.5	557.0	557.9	580.2	592.4	615.7
Farm	371.9	360.8	359.2	424.1	370.8	452.3	414.5
Total	5122.7	5282.1	5322.3	5704.3	5660.0	6166.7	6299.7

Economic Sector	1957	1958	1959	1960	1961	1962	1963
Mining	71.6	63.7	71.6	71.2	71.0	77.1	78.7
Construction	254.5	241.4	273.7	273.8	288.1	291.1	298.1
Manufacturing	1949.1	1921.3	2151.9	2171.3	2315.7	2564.3	2694.8
Trade	1151.1	1084.9	1171.2	1192.0	1219.0	1307.9	1372.8
Finance, Insurance and Real Estate	705.0	668.1	721.7	777.0	818.3	896.4	938.9
Transportation, Communication and Public Utilities	541.7	522.2	552.4	561.4	577.1	618.3	663.1
Services	624.8	641.5	667.5	680.7	705.6	736.2	759.3
Government	639.8	662.2	670.1	676.5	702.6	728.0	756.2
Farm	369.4	394.5	426.3	391.9	441.8	400.3	449.8
Total	6307.0	6199.8	6706.4	6795.8	7139.2	7619.6	8011.7

Economic Sector	1964	1965	1966	1967	1968	1969	1970
Mining	83.0	88.3	92.0	97.5	100.2	100.1	104.1
Construction	310.1	336.6	382.4	349.7	355.6	352.4	321.0
Manufacturing	3000.7	3306.5	3667.2	3726.3	4197.7	4169.4	4644.4
Trade	1466.4	1599.4	1737.7	1783.2	1868.5	1949.1	1957.5
Finance, Insurance and Real Estate	1001.9	1093.3	1155.8	1190.0	1244.8	1290.4	1231.3
Transportation, Communication and Public Utilities	700.4	746.1	814.6	851.4	920.5	968.3	1001.0
Services	788.3	845.0	858.7	892.1	925.8	991.3	1023.7
Government	801.2	855.9	902.8	932.9	962.9	990.0	1044.8
Farm	439.2	432.4	385.8	394.3	383.0	409.9	430.6
Total	8591.2	9303.5	9997.0	10217.4	10959.0	11220.9	11758.4

Appendix Tables

APPENDIX TABLE XXIII

REAL GROSS STATE PRODUCT, ALABAMA, 1950-70

(Millions of 1958 Dollars)

Economic Sector	1950	1951	1952	1953	1954	1955	1956
Mining	161.1	157.5	149.1	144.7	119.8	131.3	142.1
Construction	161.9	207.4	228.9	177.3	179.6	208.8	263.4
Manufacturing	1277.3	1426.1	1340.8	1456.6	1355.7	1598.9	1567.3
Trade	666.0	683.1	721.0	725.0	720.2	795.3	842.8
Finance, Insurance and Real Estate	389.2	410.5	436.3	443.2	474.4	509.6	569.0
Transportation, Communication and Public Utilities	346.9	395.4	397.8	407.8	407.6	414.6	437.5
Services	371.4	384.1	387.3	407.0	402.1	442.7	476.2
Government	487.9	556.7	600.5	618.0	625.4	645.9	687.4
Farm	311.9	297.5	311.6	391.6	300.8	471.3	356.2
Total	4173.6	4518.3	4573.3	4771.2	4585.6	5218.2	5343.9

Economic Sector	1957	1958	1959	1960	1961	1962	1963
Mining	149.0	127.6	139.1	153.3	137.6	124.7	113.5
Construction	272.3	241.4	249.6	243.9	225.2	212.6	222.6
Manufacturing	1598.8	1496.4	1590.3	1639.7	1594.2	1763.6	1878.0
Trade	845.4	843.4	917.6	922.8	930.0	986.6	1031.8
Finance, Insurance and Real Estate	577.8	572.6	621.5	606.3	618.6	660.6	700.3
Transportation, Communication and Public Utilities	451.5	452.1	485.4	501.6	512.9	541.4	577.2
Services	483.5	513.2	537.4	542.4	560.8	571.2	602.8
Government	719.9	742.8	766.9	794.2	824.1	833.7	844.7
Farm	299.0	329.2	356.6	358.1	355.1	332.4	409.7
Total	5397.2	5318.7	5664.4	5762.3	5758.5	6027.0	6380.6

Economic Sector	1964	1965	1966	1967	1968	1969	1970
Mining	122.0	122.3	119.6	132.3	129.1	142.7	153.1
Construction	270.6	290.5	310.7	275.8	270.8	271.5	251.8
Manufacturing	2097.6	2356.2	2676.0	2683.4	2980.2	3102.3	3355.5
Trade	1112.5	1196.4	1269.6	1291.5	1343.3	1388.0	1415.9
Finance, Insurance and Real Estate	742.8	804.8	846.4	888.0	911.2	913.2	869.5
Transportation, Communication and Public Utilities	614.0	647.9	706.0	727.3	780.3	814.8	840.2
Services	653.4	717.0	700.8	717.6	729.7	759.3	769.1
Government	863.0	890.0	952.4	982.1	1000.6	1016.4	1040.7
Farm	400.1	388.6	315.5	322.8	336.0	304.7	367.2
Total	6876.0	7413.7	7897.0	8020.8	8481.2	8712.9	9063.0

APPENDIX TABLE XXIV

REAL GROSS STATE PRODUCT, MISSISSIPPI, 1950-70

(Millions of 1958 Dollars)

Economic Sector	1950	1951	1952	1953	1954	1955	1956
Mining	26.4	29.8	35.6	34.7	39.2	44.5	49.9
Construction	96.8	119.0	100.2	99.7	97.4	103.0	100.8
Manufacturing	414.4	468.4	476.4	515.4	507.3	626.0	588.6
Trade	403.4	412.8	433.2	429.5	431.0	462.0	478.3
Finance, Insurance and Real Estate	166.2	172.3	179.5	205.3	219.1	224.5	246.8
Transportation, Communication and Public Utilities	162.3	183.8	183.7	189.6	202.9	209.2	223.6
Services	220.4	232.0	233.5	232.0	253.2	254.7	273.5
Government	270.6	269.7	275.1	280.3	292.5	298.3	317.9
Farm	401.9	351.1	435.6	495.6	397.3	546.4	435.3
Total	2162.4	2238.9	2352.8	2482.1	2434.9	2768.6	2714.7

Economic Sector	1957	1958	1959	1960	1961	1962	1963
Mining	60.0	65.8	84.2	88.5	89.0	92.9	101.9
Construction	100.2	123.6	130.5	118.0	124.8	122.9	133.4
Manufacturing	600.9	584.4	656.4	665.8	695.9	784.7	875.7
Trade	457.3	452.9	491.5	497.4	499.4	537.3	561.3
Finance, Insurance and Real Estate	258.2	258.4	285.6	293.6	322.7	342.1	365.4
Transportation, Communication and Public Utilities	229.4	224.3	242.7	298.9	257.4	276.4	288.5
Services	280.5	287.5	295.3	305.0	313.1	326.9	333.0
Government	332.0	346.2	354.9	368.0	389.7	416.6	411.6
Farm	348.6	333.3	454.6	422.0	503.7	451.8	604.9
Total	2667.1	2676.4	2995.7	3057.2	3195.7	3351.6	3675.7

Economic Sector	1964	1965	1966	1967	1968	1969	1970
Mining	99.0	92.7	94.3	102.3	106.8	114.9	115.9
Construction	135.3	160.7	174.6	163.6	148.0	156.0	150.2
Manufacturing	952.0	1028.8	1266.6	1276.2	1464.3	1401.6	1644.9
Trade	595.3	649.0	697.9	715.2	745.9	770.1	778.4
Finance, Insurance and Real Estate	381.0	417.5	451.1	476.0	495.2	498.7	474.0
Transportation, Communication and Public Utilities	307.9	373.1	353.0	368.4	399.6	426.4	435.6
Services	341.5	383.0	376.2	386.5	398.0	420.7	416.6
Government	418.4	442.4	480.8	507.3	526.2	538.6	551.7
Farm	578.4	533.8	411.8	482.3	489.6	453.8	521.3
Total	3808.8	4081.0	4306.3	4477.8	4773.6	4780.8	5088.6

Appendix Tables

APPENDIX TABLE XXV

REAL GROSS STATE PRODUCT, ARKANSAS, 1950-70

(Millions of 1958 Dollars)

Economic Sector	1950	1951	1952	1953	1954	1955	1956
Mining	59.5	63.9	69.0	65.3	64.0	69.8	70.1
Construction	104.1	146.7	150.5	121.4	91.2	91.1	85.7
Manufacturing	406.8	460.6	450.5	480.3	490.1	634.9	629.1
Trade	383.3	394.6	410.5	410.0	402.6	437.4	447.3
Finance, Insurance and Real Estate	181.7	182.6	194.0	200.6	209.9	220.3	230.0
Transportation, Communication, and Public Utilities	202.9	227.7	227.3	226.9	258.4	239.9	249.6
Services	204.4	208.9	207.4	211.8	207.2	221.9	231.7
Government	220.0	227.3	237.5	237.9	244.3	247.3	261.7
Farm	361.4	358.2	371.3	410.7	391.6	511.4	455.6
Total	2124.1	2270.5	2318.0	2364.9	2359.3	2674.0	2660.8

Economic Sector	1957	1958	1959	1960	1961	1962	1963
Mining	75.5	67.7	69.5	64.8	68.7	62.9	67.2
Construction	102.4	99.9	103.1	112.5	130.3	147.6	150.1
Manufacturing	641.5	533.7	630.9	635.2	673.8	745.7	849.9
Trade	447.1	454.4	484.5	487.5	503.7	551.5	589.7
Finance, Insurance and Real Estate	245.9	262.6	277.9	291.5	307.4	346.0	369.4
Transportation, Communication and Public Utilities	247.4	251.2	275.3	279.7	318.1	340.2	345.9
Services	241.1	254.2	265.3	271.1	283.1	304.1	316.1
Government	282.9	299.9	298.1	297.8	306.3	314.7	319.2
Farm	369.2	357.1	499.7	459.7	533.0	508.9	531.7
Total	2653.0	2580.7	2904.3	2899.8	3124.4	3321.6	3539.2

Economic Sector	1964	1965	1966	1967	1968	1969	1970
Mining	69.1	68.0	76.0	79.1	77.9	80.8	78.5
Construction	142.9	163.4	178.0	167.5	155.3	144.2	126.2
Manufacturing	950.3	1031.9	1210.1	1242.3	1441.4	1506.1	1696.5
Trade	635.1	667.5	686.6	711.1	755.1	772.6	782.1
Finance, Insurance and Real Estate	400.0	436.7	455.0	476.0	492.0	504.9	485.2
Transportation, Communication and Public Utilities	379.1	395.3	426.7	435.2	464.0	475.2	491.0
Services	334.4	345.0	331.1	351.6	368.1	393.1	400.4
Government	322.6	362.8	391.5	398.9	414.0	431.1	438.6
Farm	629.1	537.1	539.8	498.0	521.5	593.3	508.0
Total	3862.6	4007.7	4294.8	4359.7	4689.3	4901.3	5006.5

APPENDIX TABLE XXVI

REAL GROSS STATE PRODUCT, LOUISIANA, 1950-70

(Millions of 1958 Dollars)

Economic Sector	1950	1951	1952	1953	1954	1955	1956
Mining	282.3	304.6	348.8	377.3	431.8	524.9	596.2
Construction	247.3	285.0	299.7	341.3	320.7	300.0	350.3
Manufacturing	1177.5	1285.5	1280.8	1324.4	1240.4	1532.1	1554.9
Trade	788.2	787.6	824.0	859.1	896.1	982.0	1035.3
Finance, Insurance and Real Estate	426.0	451.0	480.0	513.2	552.0	583.1	623.4
Transportation, Communication and Public Utilities	517.3	591.3	615.5	631.0	652.6	688.9	743.1
Services	495.4	496.1	494.7	503.8	506.4	552.4	587.6
Government	497.6	522.3	525.9	544.4	571.0	599.5	631.8
Farm	233.2	260.3	287.7	322.7	279.6	318.4	285.5
Total	4664.8	4983.7	5157.1	5417.2	5450.6	6081.3	6408.1

Economic Sector	1957	1958	1959	1960	1961	1962	1963
Mining	630.5	609.9	664.0	662.9	701.7	738.7	777.6
Construction	420.7	401.1	370.0	332.8	316.9	313.8	328.6
Manufacturing	1518.7	1284.0	1362.3	1360.6	1382.5	1474.5	1623.4
Trade	1094.8	1094.9	1162.3	1149.7	1136.2	1204.0	1266.3
Finance, Insurance and Real Estate	684.3	719.8	748.7	765.7	779.9	809.9	854.1
Transportation, Communication and Public Utilities	787.3	755.4	793.2	814.1	827.2	868.3	926.9
Services	631.1	624.9	653.9	654.8	664.6	691.7	703.7
Government	659.5	673.0	685.2	708.6	733.6	753.5	772.4
Farm	250.4	234.9	293.6	275.9	311.6	297.9	372.8
Total	6677.3	6397.9	6733.2	6725.1	6854.2	7152.3	7625.8

Economic Sector	1964	1965	1966	1967	1968	1969	1970
Mining	836.4	892.3	973.6	1068.5	1084.8	1158.0	1044.4
Construction	382.4	441.5	542.4	539.0	550.2	466.6	428.5
Manufacturing	1765.4	1932.1	2180.7	2171.4	2423.3	2335.7	2588.0
Trade	1358.3	1488.0	1612.9	1661.9	1755.8	1810.8	1818.8
Finance, Insurance and Real Estate	914.2	1002.1	1077.6	1112.0	1139.1	1156.4	1099.4
Transportation, Communication and Public Utilities	1012.2	1070.5	1138.6	1229.2	1312.5	1364.0	1391.9
Services	752.5	796.1	790.1	832.0	858.1	916.3	927.4
Government	795.2	838.1	904.5	963.0	985.1	1016.2	1040.2
Farm	365.5	320.6	313.7	334.0	409.0	336.1	386.5
Total	8182.1	8781.3	9534.1	9910.7	10517.9	10560.1	10725.1

APPENDIX TABLE XXVII

REAL PRODUCT PER EMPLOYEE, UNITED STATES AND SOUTHEAST, 1950, 1960, and 1970

(1958 Dollars)

Economic Sector	United States			Southeast		
	1950	1960	1970	1950	1960	1970
Private Nonfarm	$ 7628	$ 9054	$10866	$ 6655	$ 7852	$ 9840
Mining	11876	18399	27653	7791	12197	19109
Construction	6944	7522	7055	5614	5837	5342
Manufacturing	6922	8389	11245	6224	7172	10300
Trade	6435	7225	8498	5488	6159	7751
Finance, Insurance and Real Estate	21365	24016	25908	21006	21593	23379
Transportation, Communication and Public Utilities	7635	11214	17185	7017	10397	15560
Services	6392	6601	6251	5901	6316	6024

APPENDIX TABLE XXVIII

REAL PRODUCT PER EMPLOYEE, SOUTHEASTERN STATES, 1950, 1960, and 1970

(1958 Dollars)

Economic Sector	Virginia			West Virginia		
	1950	1960	1970	1950	1960	1970
Private Nonfarm	$ 7053	$ 8144	$ 9829	$ 7168	$ 8939	$11600
Mining	6856	9506	17830	7845	12426	20108
Construction	5412	5781	5277	5713	6598	6622
Manufacturing	7059	7526	10099	7842	9610	13286
Trade	5588	6287	7842	5116	5851	7487
Finance, Insurance and Real Estate	20853	22874	24131	19535	21053	21070
Transportation, Communication and Public Utilities	7298	10909	16366	6801	9986	14954
Services	6199	6831	6216	5409	5346	5525

Economic Sector	North Carolina			South Carolina		
	1950	1960	1970	1950	1960	1970
Private Nonfarm	$ 5997	$ 6979	$ 9155	$ 5500	$ 6520	$ 8527
Mining	6471	9818	14128	9333	9438	13882
Construction	5754	4952	4608	4399	4827	4272
Manufacturing	5383	6277	9456	4964	5737	8370
Trade	5682	6198	7715	4988	5411	7261
Finance, Insurance and Real Estate	19478	20952	22399	20382	18427	21815
Transportation, Communication and Public Utilities	6898	9833	14717	6204	9549	14432
Services	5576	6028	5589	5649	6467	6598

APPENDIX TABLE XXVIII Cont.

Economic Sector	Georgia			Florida		
	1950	1960	1970	1950	1960	1970
Private Nonfarm	$ 6125	$ 7646	$ 9709	$ 7224	$ 8427	$ 9953
Mining	6833	10036	15667	7484	12447	16209
Construction	5886	5656	5225	5499	6306	5698
Manufacturing	5195	6412	8738	6029	8021	11069
Trade	5656	6458	8401	5303	6004	7618
Finance, Insurance and Real Estate	20150	21054	24105	27197	24073	25818
Transportation, Communication and Public Utilities	7162	10773	16121	7451	10891	16258
Services	4856	6590	6420	6997	6794	6345

Economic Sector	Kentucky			Tennessee		
	1950	1960	1970	1950	1960	1970
Private Nonfarm	$ 7867	$ 9153	$11555	$ 6537	$ 7351	$ 9334
Mining	7473	10671	19350	6880	9753	14871
Construction	6808	7226	6729	5697	5850	5087
Manufacturing	9348	10431	14442	6508	6880	9997
Trade	5991	6692	8211	5292	6144	7570
Finance, Insurance and Real Estate	19748	22076	23480	19536	19579	21526
Transportation, Communication and Public Utilities	7481	10834	16176	7241	10152	15144
Services	5916	5983	5596	5210	5654	5531

Economic Sector	Alabama			Mississippi		
	1950	1960	1970	1950	1960	1970
Private Nonfarm	$ 6469	$ 7475	$ 9558	$ 6027	$ 7163	$ 9000
Mining	6685	11792	18446	10154	13209	17831
Construction	5741	5646	5118	5728	5244	4622
Manufacturing	5911	6919	10363	4796	5553	9053
Trade	5527	6119	7425	5496	5886	7316
Finance, Insurance and Real Estate	19657	18655	20952	19786	21748	22464
Transportation, Communication and Public Utilities	6842	10012	15112	6340	11768	14569
Services	5981	6020	5835	6501	6932	6117

Economic Sector	Arkansas			Louisiana		
	1950	1960	1970	1950	1960	1970
Private Nonfarm	$ 6251	$ 7201	$ 9407	$ 7364	$ 8906	$11225
Mining	9015	11782	17444	10118	15032	20600
Construction	5720	5542	4891	5262	6062	5806
Manufacturing	5374	6209	10110	8121	9582	14755
Trade	5383	5996	7357	5555	6300	7908
Finance, Insurance and Real Estate	21631	21754	22673	19907	21815	22575
Transportation, Communication and Public Utilities	6763	9954	15154	6649	9726	15031
Services	5569	5818	5455	6768	6401	5899

Notes

CHAPTER I

1. The Southeast in this study is defined according to the U.S. Department of Commerce concept; this includes Virginia, West Virginia, North Carolina, South Carolina, Georgia, Florida, Kentucky, Tennessee, Alabama, Mississippi, Arkansas, and Louisiana.

2. The personal income estimates are generally published annually in the August issue of the *Survey of Current Business*, published by the U.S. Department of Commerce. Personal income includes the net interest paid by governments and consumers plus transfer payments; each of these items is excluded from gross product.

3. See John W. Kendrick and C. Milton Jaycox, "The Concept and Estimation of Gross State Product," *Southern Economic Journal*, October 1965; the Kendrick-Jaycox estimation procedure is explained later in this chapter.

4. I have made the following applications of the Kendrick-Jaycox estimation procedure: *Georgia: Gross State Product and Productivity, 1950-1968* (Division of Research, College of Business Administration, University of Georgia, 1971); "Georgia's Gross State Product," *Georgia Business*, October 1970; "Georgia's Gross State Product, 1950-1971," *Georgia Business*, May 1973; and "New England: Gross State Product and Productivity, 1948-1965" (Ph.D. dissertation, University of Connecticut, 1969).

In addition, see the following: W. L. L'Esperance, G. Nestel, and D. Fromm, "Gross State Product and an Econometric Model of a State," *Journal of the American Statistical Association*, September 1969; E. John Fromelt, "Gross State Product Estimates for South Dakota," *South Dakota Business Review*, May 1972; Gary A. Lynch, "Estimating Idaho and Regional Gross Product," *Idaho Business and Economic Review*, June 1971; and Philip F. Rice and R. Wayne Gober, "Louisiana Gross State Product," *The Louisiana Economy*, May 1973.

5. Harry Oshima and his associates at the Economic Research Center, University of Hawaii, have had a great deal of success in measuring net exports for the insular economy of Hawaii; see Harry T. Oshima and Mitsuo Ono, *Hawaii's Income and Expenditures, 1958, 1959, and 1960*, 3 vols. (Honolulu: Economic Research Center, University of Hawaii, January 1965), and Yung C. Shang, William H. Albrecht, and Glenn Ifuku, *Hawaii's Income and Expenditure Accounts, 1958-1968* (Honolulu: Economic Research Center, University of Hawaii, July 1970).

6. See the following: Karen R. Polenske et al., *State Estimates of the Gross National Product, 1947, 1958, 1963* (Lexington, Mass.: D. C. Heath and Co., 1972); John M. Rodgers, *State Estimates of Outputs, Employment, and Payrolls, 1947, 1958, 1963* (Lexington, Mass.: D. C. Heath and Co., 1972); and Raymond C. Scheppach, Jr., *State Projections of the Gross National Product, 1970, 1980* (Lexington, Mass.: D. C. Heath and Co., 1972).

For a discussion of the difficulties encountered in the above studies in measuring state and regional exports and imports, see Polenske et al., *State Estimates of the Gross National Product*, chap. 4, and Scheppach, *State Projections of the Gross National Product*, chap. 4.

7. Harold K. Charlesworth and William G. Herzel, *The Gross State Product of Kentucky: 1968* (Lexington: Office of Development Services and Business Research, College of Business and Economics, University of Kentucky, 1972).

8. A full discussion of the assumptions involved in this author's method is provided below.

9. In the final report by Charlesworth and Herzel on the Kentucky gross state product, the figures were only provided in current dollars and were not deflated. As a result, their gross state product figures are not conducive to measuring economic growth.

10. J. Thomas Romans, *Capital Exports and Growth among U.S. Regions* (Middletown, Conn.: Wesleyan University Press, 1965).

11. Detailed systems of economic accounts have been developed in the following studies: W. R. Maki, J. R. Barnard, and R. E. Suttor, *Simulation of Regional Product and Income with Emphasis on Iowa, 1954-1974*, Iowa Agricultural Experiment Station Research Bulletin 548 (Ames: Iowa State University of Science and Technology, 1966); Jerald R. Barnard, *Design and Use of Social Accounting Systems in State Development Planning* (Iowa City: Bureau of Business and Economic Research, University of Iowa, 1967); William L. Anthes, "Gross State Product for Arkansas, 1958 and 1963," *Arkansas Business and Economic Review*, February 1969; Kalman Goldberg, *A System of Gross Income and Product Accounts for Illinois, 1963* (Springfield, Ill.: Department of Economic and Business Development, State of Illinois, 1967); Oshima and Ono, *Hawaii's Income and Expenditures*; and Shang, Albrecht, and Ifuku, *Hawaii's Income and Expenditure Accounts*.

12. Walter Isard, "Regional Commodity Balances and Interregional Commodity Flow," *American Economic Review*, May 1953, and Frederick T. Moore and James W. Petersen, "Regional Analysis: An Interindustry Model of Utah," *Review of Economics and Statistics*, November 1955.

13. See the following for examples of state input-output models: Curtis C. Harris, Jr., *A 1970 Interindustry Model of the State of Maryland* (College Park: Bureau of Business and Economic Research, University of Maryland, October 1971); A. David Sandoval, "A Development Strategy for New Mexico: 1961-1980," *New Mexico Business*, October 1970; Philip J. Bourque et al., *The Washington Economy: An Input-Output Study* (Seattle: The Graduate School of Business Administration, University of Washington, 1967); Anilkumar G. Tijoriwala, William F. Martin, and Leonard G. Bower, *Structure of the Arizona Economy* (Tucson: Agricultural Experiment Station, The University of Arizona, November 1968); I. E. Bradley, "Utah Interindustry Study," *Utah Economic and Business Review*, 1967; Charles H. Little and Gerald Doekson, *An Input-Output Analysis of Oklahoma's Economy*, Technical Bulletin T-124 (Stillwater: Oklahoma Agricultural Experiment Station, February 1968); M. J. Emerson et al., *The Interindustry Structure of the Kansas Economy* (Topeka: State of Kansas, 1969); Herbert W. Grubb and William G. Lesso, "The Input-Output Model for the State of Texas," *Texas Business Review*, January 1974; Jerald R. Barnard and Harold K. Charlesworth, *The Structure of the Kentucky Economy: An Input-Output Study* (Lexington: College of Business and Economics, University of Kentucky, 1970); Tong Hun Lee, John R. Moore, and David P. Lewis, *A Report on the Tennessee Interindustry Study* (Knoxville: College of Business Administration, University of Tennessee, December 1967); R. D. Peterson and R. A. Wykstra, "A Provisional Input-Output Study of Idaho's Economy," *University of Washington Business Review*, Winter 1968; Robert L. Allen and Donald A. Watson, *The Structure of the Oregon Economy: An Input-Output Study* (Eugene: Bureau of Business and Economic Research, University of Oregon, 1965); William A. Schaffer, Eugene A. Laurent, and Ernest M. Sutter, Jr., *Introducing the Georgia Economic Model* (Atlanta: The Georgia Department of Industry and Trade, 1972); Floyd K. Harmston and Claude E. Monroe, *The Inter-Industry Structure of Missouri, 1958*

(Columbia: Research Center, School of Business and Public Administration, University of Missouri, 1967); John G. D. Carden and F. B. Whittington, Jr., *Studies in the Economic Structure of the State of Mississippi* (Jackson: Mississippi Industrial and Technological Research Commission, 1964); William H. Miernyk et al., *Simulating Regional Economic Development* (Lexington, Mass.: D. C. Heath and Co., 1970); and Teddy T. Su, *The South Carolina Economy: An Input-Output Study* (Columbia: Bureau of Business and Economic Research, University of South Carolina, 1970).

14. For a clear statement of the conceptual and data problems involved in regional input-output analysis, see the following: Charles M. Tiebout, "Regional and Interregional Input-Output Models: An Appraisal," *Southern Economic Journal*, October 1957; Teddy T. Su, "A Note on Regional Input-Output Models," *Southern Economic Journal*, January 1970; and William H. Miernyk, *The Elements of Input-Output Analysis* (New York: Random House, 1966), pp. 58-77.

15. An example of the forecasting possibilities of a gross state product series was provided by L'Esperance, Nestel, and Fromm, "Gross State Product and an Econometric Model of a State."

16. See *Growth and Change*, April 1972, for the argument for a gross state product series by Donald Ratajczak and Robert M. Williams in "The Case for a Gross State Product Series," and a more conservative view regarding gross state product estimation by Robert E. Graham, Jr., in "The View from Washington."

17. Active projects involving the construction of state econometric models are currently underway in Georgia and Kentucky.

18. Harold T. Moody, Frank W. Puffer, and Robert M. Williams, "An Eight Region Model," *Growth and Change*, October 1970.

19. See Polenske et al., *State Estimates of the Gross National Product*, Rodgers, *State Estimates of Outputs, Employment and Payrolls*, and Scheppach, *State Projections of the Gross National Product*.

20. For example, the national ratio of supplements to wages and salaries for 1970 was calculated from table 1.13, U.S. Department of Commerce, *Survey of Current Business*, July 1971. For a given year o, where S = supplements, WS = wages and salaries, GGP = gross government product, and n and s represent nation and state respectively, the procedure is as follows:

$$(S/WS)_n^o \cdot (WS)_s^o = S_s^o$$

$$(WS)_s^o + S_s^o = GGP_s^o$$

The state wage and salary data for government are available in the August issue of the *Survey of Current Business*; for 1970, see *Survey of Current Business*, August 1971, pp. 32-36.

21. The relevant data for the agricultural sector are compiled in U.S. Department of Agriculture, Economic Research Service, *Farm Income, State Estimates, 1959-1971*, A Supplement to the July 1972 Farm Income Situation, August 1972. Data for the earlier years were taken from U.S. Department of Agriculture, Economic Research Service, *Farm Income, State Estimates, 1949-1964*, A Supplement to the July 1965 Farm Income Situation, August 1965.

22. The historical series on G.N.P. by major industry, including disaggregation of capital consumption allowances and indirect business taxes, appeared in Jack J. Gottsegen, "Revised Estimates of G.N.P. by Major Industries," *Survey of Current Business*, April 1967. This series is updated in each year's July issue of the *Survey of Current Business*; for 1970 see table 1.22, *Survey of Current Business*, July 1971, p. 21.

23. The historical series on income received is available from the Department of

Commerce on an unpublished basis. In recent years, the figures have appeared in the August issue of the *Survey of Current Business*; for 1970, see table 70, *Survey of Current Business*, August 1971, p. 37.

24. National coefficients for 1970 were calculated from the following sources: income received, table 70, *Survey of Current Business*, August 1971, p. 37; income originating (national income), table 1.12, *Survey of Current Business*, July 1971, p. 17; capital consumption allowances and indirect business taxes, table 1.22, *Survey of Current Business*, July 1971, p. 21.

25. It would be possible to program the Kendrick-Jaycox estimation procedure and generate gross state product figures by use of a computer; however, the procedure is also easily performed on an electronic calculator. In this study, I used an electronic calculator and organized the worksheets according to the format shown in exhibit A.

26. For 1970, the manufacturing adjustment was calculated from the following reports in the 1970 *Annual Survey of Manufactures: General Statistics for Industry Groups and Industries*, p. 4, and *Statistics for Divisions and States*, parts 5, 6, and 7.

27. The ratio of value added/labor payroll in North Carolina relative to the national average was calculated at 1.151 for 1970. Adjusted gross manufacturing output was calculated as follows:

$$(1.151) \quad (\$6807.0 \text{ million}) \quad = \quad \$7834.9 \text{ million}$$

where $6807.0 million represents the unadjusted estimate of manufacturing output shown in exhibit A.

28. The historical series on industry deflators appeared in the article by Gottsegen, "Revised Estimates of G.N.P. by Major Industries," table 4, p. 24. Price data for more recent years have been published in the April issues of the *Survey of Current Business* and in the July 1972 issue of the *Survey of Current Business*, table 1.21, p. 23.

29. Farm prices are obtained from the U.S. Department of Agriculture, *Agricultural Statistics*.

30. Albert W. Niemi, Jr., "A Re-Examination of the Kendrick-Jaycox Method of Estimating Gross State Product," *Review of Regional Studies*, Spring 1972.

CHAPTER II

1. For an excellent description of the various productivity measures see Solomon Fabricant, *Basic Facts on Productivity Change*, (New York: Occasional Paper No. 63, National Bureau of Economic Research, 1959). Also see the following: John W. Kendrick, *Productivity Trends in the United States* (Princeton: Princeton University Press, 1961); John W. Kendrick, "Productivity Trends: Capital and Labor," *Review of Economics and Statistics*, August 1956.

2. Substitution of capital for labor does not appear to have been a major factor in labor productivity advance. Kendrick, "Productivity Trends: Capital and Labor," found that in most industries, during 1889-1953, capital substituted for labor at 0.1-0.3% and was not a major source of labor productivity advance. Robert M. Solow, "Technical Change and the Aggregate Production Function," *Review of Economics and Statistics*, August 1957, argued that almost 90% of the increase in labor productivity reflected technological improvements, and only slightly more than 10% of the increase could be attributed to substitution of capital for labor.

3. The description of the estimation procedure followed in this study (chap. 1) explained why it is impossible to calculate productivity change for the government sector. For agriculture, it is difficult to obtain accurate estimates of the full-time labor force, and, therefore, no measure of productivity has been attempted for this sector.

4. Kendrick, *Productivity Trends*, pointed to an upswing in the long-run rate of productivity growth dating from World War I.

CHAPTER IV

1. The exchange of views concerning regional per capita movements took place in the *Southern Economic Journal*. See the following: Stephen L. McDonald, "On the South's Recent Economic Development," July 1961; Rufus B. Hughes, Jr., "Interregional Income Differences: Self Perpetuation," July 1961; E. J. R. Booth, "Interregional Income Differences," July 1964.

2. Stephen McDonald argued the case for the South's convergence toward parity with national per capita income. Rufus Hughes, on the other hand, argued that per capita differences tend to be self perpetuating.

3. Booth used the Commerce Department's regional and national estimates of per capita income and computed the rest of the United States as the per capita income of the non-South. My analysis is not comparable to Booth's since I am comparing the Southeast and the southeastern states to the national average per capita output. Also, since my analysis concerns per capita production rather than per capita income, comparisons should not be made with earlier results.

4. The linear equation was of the standard form, $Y = a + bX$, where $Y =$ the absolute or relative measure of per capita output differences and $X =$ time, running in years from 0 to 20. The logarithmic equation was of the form, $\log Y = a + bX$.

5. In other words, the trend in per capita output in the state (b_s) must exceed the trend in per capita output in the nation (b_n) and the difference $(b_s - b_n)$ must be significantly different from zero.

6. There are great limitations and risks involved in extrapolation. The estimates provided in this study provide a solid foundation for study of per capita output movements for the past two decades, but whether these trends can be extrapolated three or four decades into the future is very doubtful. The past two decades have witnessed the most significant improvement in the standard of living that the American economy has ever experienced; this is especially true in the Southeast. To extrapolate into the future on the basis of the past two decades assumes that this unprecedented growth will continue. Past history and the recent development of an energy shortage should make one very cautious about accepting such an assumption. To highlight the problems involved in extrapolation, it should be pointed out that the prediction that the Southeast will attain parity with the national average per capita output level in 40 years is subject to a high margin of error ($\pm$ 15 years). It should also be made clear that since the Southeast is included in the national average, the above calculations tend to overstate the time required for convergence with the non-Southeast.

7. South Carolina's decline compared to the regional average was not statistically significant.

CHAPTER V

1. Edward F. Denison, "United States Economic Growth," *Journal of Business*, April 1962.

2. John W. Kendrick, *Productivity Trends in the United States* (Princeton: Princeton University Press, 1961), p. 14.

3. John W. Kendrick, "Productivity Trends: Capital and Labor," *Review of Economics and Statistics*, August 1956, p. 10.

4. Robert M. Solow, "Technical Change and the Aggregate Production Function," *Review of Economics and Statistics*, August 1957.

5. F. C. Mills, "The Role of Productivity in Economic Growth," *American Economic Review*, May 1952.

6. Theodore M. Schultz, "Investment in Human Capital," *American Economic Review*, May 1960.

7. See Mills, "The Role of Productivity in Economic Growth."

8. The calculation of the productivity increment in this study includes substitution of capital for labor as an improvement in the efficiency of labor utilization. However, two studies (Kendrick, "Productivity Trends: Capital and Labor," and Solow, "Technical Change and the Aggregate Production Function,") indicated that factor substitution has been a rather minor source of labor productivity increase.

9. Real government output in the absence of productivity change is taken simply as the original estimate of real gross government product, since this was estimated on the assumption of constant productivity in government. The estimate of real farm product in the absence of productivity change was calculated by using the average percentage increase in real product with no productivity change for the aggregate of all private nonfarm industries. Since agriculture is such a small sector, any bias introduced by this assumption would tend to be insignificant.

CHAPTER VI

1. Glenn E. McLaughlin and Stefan Robock, Why Industry Moves South (Washington, D.C.: National Planning Association, Committee of the South, 1949); Harvey S. Perloff et al., Regions, Resources, and Economic Growth (Baltimore: The Johns Hopkins Press, 1960); and Victor R. Fuchs, Changes in the Location of Manufacturing in the United States since 1929 (New Haven: Yale University Press, 1962).

2. See McLaughlin and Robock, Why Industry Moves South, chap. 3. An excellent summary of Perloff et al.'s study is provided by Leonard F. Wheat, Regional Growth and Industrial Location (Lexington, Mass.: Lexington Books, D. C. Heath and Company, 1970), chap. 1.

3. See McLaughlin and Robock, Why Industry Moves South, chap. 3.

4. See Fuchs, Changes in Location of Manufacturing, chap. 4.

5. See Wheat, Regional Growth and Industrial Location, chaps. 1, 2, and 7.

6. Wheat qualifies his argument concerning the effects of agglomeration by pointing out that some external economies may get captured in market effects.

7. William E. Morgan, "The Effects of State and Local Tax and Financial Inducements on Industrial Location" (Ph.D. dissertation, University of Colorado, 1964), chaps. 3 and 4.

8. See the Fantus Company, The Appalachian Location Research Studies Program (New York: Fantus Company, Fantus Area Research Division, 1966).

9. Thomas P. Bergin and William F. Eagan, "Economic Growth and Community Facilities," Municipal Finance, May 1961.

10. A. Lee Cobb, "Factors Affecting Industrial Location in Georgia," Georgia Business, May 1957; Melvin L. Greenhut, "An Empirical Model and a Survey: New Plant Locations in Florida," Review of Economics and Statistics, November 1959.

11. McLaughlin and Robock, Why Industry Moves South, chap. 4.

12. U.S. Bureau of the Census, Census of the United States: 1970, Detailed Characteristics, United States Summary, table 347.

13. The South Atlantic region is defined as including Delaware, Maryland, the District of Columbia, Virginia, West Virginia, North Carolina, South Carolina, Georgia, and Florida; the East South Central region is defined as including Kentucky, Tennessee, Alabama, and Mississippi; and the West South Central region is defined as including Arkansas, Louisiana, Oklahoma, and Texas. Throughout this chapter, the South refers to all states in the South Atlantic, East South Central, and West South Central regions; the non-South refers to the remainder of the United States.

14. U.S. Bureau of the Census, Statistical Abstract of the United States, 1972, table 390.

15. Ibid., table 396.

16. See McLaughlin and Robock, Why Industry Moves South, chap. 6.

17. For an excelllent summary of educational trends in the South, see James G.

Maddox et al., *The Advancing South* (New York: The Twentieth Century Fund, 1967), and Marshall R. Colberg, *Human Capital in Southern Development, 1939-1963* (Chapel Hill: University of North Carolina Press, 1965).
18. Census, *Statistical Abstract*, 1971, table 413.
19. James S. Coleman et al., *Equality of Educational Opportunity* (Washington, D.C.: U.S. Department of Health, Education, and Welfare, Office of Education, 1966).
20. There has been criticism of the Coleman report's analysis of achievement test results, but the concern has centered on the interpretation of the source of the results and not on the magnitude of the racial or regional differences. Maddox et al., *The Advancing South*, chap. 5, provide several interesting measures of regional quality variation in education, particularly in regards to blacks vs. whites.
21. For summary figures on average salaries of teachers and average expenditures per pupil see Census, *Statistical Abstract*, 1972, tables 191 and 194.
22. Maddox et al., *The Advancing South*, chap. 7; Colberg, *Human Capital*, chaps. 7 and 8.
23. See McLaughlin and Robock, *Why Industry Moves South*, chap. 6; Calvin B. Hoover and B. U. Ratchford, *Economic Resources and Policies of the South* (New York: The Macmillan Company, 1951), chap. 15.
24. See Maddox et al., *The Advancing South*, chap. 4.
25. See Wheat, *Regional Growth and Industrial Location*, chap. 7.
26. See ibid., chap. 1.
27. See Fuchs, *Changing Location of Manufacturing*, chap. 6.
28. See ibid., chaps. 1 and 7.
29. The deflation was based on the wholesale commodity prices provided in each issue of the *Monthly Labor Review* (also see Census, *Statistical Abstract*, 1971, table 531).
30. The residual of 23.9% was produced in industries that were not designated as either capital or labor intensive.
31. See Wheat, *Regional Growth and Industrial Location*, chap. 2.
32. See Fuchs, *Changes in the Location of Manufacturing*, chap. 4.
33. Census, *Statistical Abstract*, 1971, table 1000.
34. Ibid., table 796, and U.S. Federal Power Commission, *Hydroelectric Power Resources of the United States*, 1972.
35. See Fuchs, *Changes in the Location of Manufacturing*, chap.4; Wheat, *Regional Growth and Industrial Location*, chaps. 1 and 7.
36. See Morgan, "The Effects of State and Local Tax and Financial Inducements on Industrial Location," especially chaps. 3 and 4.
37. Advisory Commission on Intergovernmental Relations, *State-Local Taxation and Industrial Location* (Washington, D.C.: Advisory Commission on Intergovernmental Relations, April 1967); William V. Williams, "A Measure of the Impact of State and Local Taxes on Industry Location," *Journal of Regional Science*, Summer 1967; and Joe S. Floyd, *Effects of Taxation on Industrial Location* (Chapel Hill: University of North Carolina Press, 1952).
38. Hoover and Ratchford, *Economic Resources and Policies*, chap. 8; McLaughlin and Robock, *Why Industry Moves South*, chap. 8.
39. See the following articles in the August 1971 issue of *Ebony*: A. A. Fletcher, "When Industry Goes South"; L. Bennett, Jr., "Old Illusions and New Souths"; and the three unsigned articles, "It's Good to Be Home Again," "Black Voices of the South," and "White Voices of the South."

Bibliography

BOOKS

Advisory Commission on Intergovernmental Relations. *State-Local Taxation and Industrial Location*. Washington: Advisory Commission on Intergovernmental Relations, April 1967.

Allen, Robert L., and Donald A. Watson. *The Structure of the Oregon Economy: An Input-Output Study*. Eugene: Bureau of Business and Economic Research, University of Oregon, 1965.

Barnard, Jerald R. *Design and Use of Social Accounting Systems in State Development Planning*. Iowa City: Bureau of Business and Economic Research, University of Iowa, 1967.

————, and Harold K. Charlesworth. *The Structure of the Kentucky Economy: An Input-Output Study*. Lexington: College of Business and Economics, University of Kentucky, 1970.

Bourque, Philip J., et al. *The Washington Economy: An Input-Output Study*. Seattle: The Graduate School of Business Administration, University of Washington, 1967.

Carden, John G. D., and F. B. Whittington, Jr. *Studies in the Economic Structure of the State of Mississippi*. Jackson: Mississippi Industrial and Technological Research Commission, 1964.

Chapman, John H., Jr., and Kenneth L. Shellhammer. *The Structure of the West Virginia Economy, 1965: A Preliminary Report*. Morgantown, W. Va.: Regional Research Institute, November 1967.

Charlesworth, Harold K., and William G. Herzel. *The Gross State Product of Kentucky: 1968*. Lexington: Office of Development Services and Business Research, College of Business and Economics, University of Kentucky, 1970.

Colberg, Marshall R. *Human Capital in Southern Development, 1939-1963*. Chapel Hill: University of North Carolina Press, 1965.

Coleman, Joseph S., et al. *Equality of Educational Opportunity*. Washington, D.C.: U.S. Department of Health, Education, and Welfare, Office of Education, 1966.

Emerson, M. J., et al. *The Interindustry Structure of the Kansas Economy*. Topeka: State of Kansas, 1969.

Fabricant, Solomon. *Basic Facts on Productivity Change*, Occasional Paper No. 63. New York: National Bureau of Economic Research, 1959.

Fantus Company. *The Appalachian Location Research Studies Program*. New York: Fantus Company, Fantus Area Research Division, 1966.

Floyd, Joe S. *Effects of Taxation on Industrial Location*. Chapel Hill: University of North Carolina Press, 1952.

Fuchs, Victor R. *Changes in the Location of Manufacturing in the United States since 1929*. New Haven: Yale University Press, 1962.

Goldberg, Kalman. *A System of Gross Income and Product Accounts for Illinois, 1963*. Springfield: Department of Economic and Business Development, State of Illinois, 1967.

Harmston, Floyd K., and Claude E. Monroe. *The Inter-Industry Structure of Missouri, 1958*. Columbia: Research Center, School of Business and Public Administration, University of Missouri, 1967.

Harris, Curtis C., Jr. *A 1970 Interindustry Model of the State of Maryland*. College Park: Bureau of Business and Economic Research, University of Maryland, October 1971.

Hoover, Calvin B., and B. U. Ratchford. *Economic Resources and Policies of the South*. New York: The Macmillan Company, 1951.

Isard, Walter. *Methods of Regional Analysis*. New York: The Technology Press of M.I.T. and John Wiley and Sons, 1960.

Kendrick, John W. *Productivity Trends in the United States*. Princeton: Princeton University Press, 1961.

Lee, Tong Hun, John R. Moore, and David P. Lewis. *A Report on the Tennessee Interindustry Study*. Knoxville: College of Business Administration, University of Tennessee, December 1967.

Little, Charles H., and Gerald Doekson. *An Input-Output Analysis of Oklahoma's Economy*, Technical Bulletin T-124. Stillwater: Oklahoma Agricultural Experiment Station, February 1968.

McLaughlin, Glenn E., and Stefan Robock. *Why Industry Moves South*. Washington, D.C.: National Planning Association, Committee of the South, 1949.

Maddox, James G., et al. *The Advancing South*. New York: The Twentieth Century Fund, 1967.

Maki, W. R., J. R. Barnard, and R. E. Suttor. *Simulation of Regional Product and Income with Emphasis on Iowa, 1954-1974*, Iowa Agricultural Experiment Station Research Bulletin 548. Ames: Iowa State University of Science and Technology, 1966.

Miernyk, William H. *The Elements of Input-Output Analysis*. New York: Random House, 1966.

―――, et al. *Simulating Regional Economic Development*. Lexington, Mass.: D. C. Heath and Co., 1970.

Morgan, William E. "The Effects of State and Local Tax and Financial Inducements on Industrial Location." Ph.D. dissertation, University of Colorado, 1964.

Niemi, Albert W., Jr. *Georgia: Gross State Product and Productivity, 1950-1968*. Athens: Division of Research, College of Business Administration, University of Georgia, 1971.

―――. "New England: Gross State Product and Productivity, 1948-1965." Ph.D. dissertation, University of Connecticut, 1969.

Oshima, Harry T., and Mitsuo Ono. *Hawaii's Income and Expenditure 1958, 1959, and 1960*. 3 vols. Honolulu: Economic Research Center, University of Hawaii, January 1965.

Perloff, Harvey S., et al. *Regions, Resources, and Economic Growth*. Baltimore: The Johns Hopkins Press, 1960.

Polenske, Karen R., et al. *State Estimates of the Gross National Product, 1947, 1958, 1963*. Lexington, Mass.: D. C. Heath and Co., 1972.

Rodgers, John M. *State Estimates of Outputs, Employment, and Payrolls, 1947, 1958, 1963*. Lexington, Mass.: D. C. Heath and Co., 1972.

Romans, J. Thomas. *Capital Exports and Growth among U.S. Regions*. Middletown, Conn.: Wesleyan University Press, 1965.

Schaffer, William A., Eugene A. Laurent, and Ernest M. Sutter, Jr. *Introducing the Georgia Economic Model*. Atlanta: The Georgia Department of Industry and Trade, 1972.

Scheppach, Raymond C., Jr. *State Projections of the Gross National Product, 1970, 1980*. Lexington, Mass.: D. C. Heath and Co., 1972.

Shang, Yung C., William H. Albrecht, and Glenn Ifuku. *Hawaii's Income and Expenditure Accounts, 1958-1968*. Honolulu: Economic Research Center, University of Hawaii, July 1970.

Su, Teddy T. *The South Carolina Economy: An Input-Output Study*. Columbia: Bureau of Business and Economic Research, University of South Carolina, 1970.

Tijoriwala, Anilkumar G., William E. Martin, and Leonard G. Bower. *Structure of the Arizona Economy*. Tucson: Agricultural Experiment Station, The University of Arizona, November 1968.

Wheat, Leonard F. *Regional Growth and Industrial Location*. Lexington, Mass.: Lexington Books, D. C. Heath and Co., 1973.

ARTICLES

Anthes, William L. "Gross State Product for Arkansas, 1958 and 1963." *Arkansas Business and Economic Review*, February 1969.

Bennett, L., Jr. "Old Illusions and New Souths." *Ebony*, August 1971.

Bergin, Thomas P., and William F. Eagan. "Economic Growth and Community Facilities." *Municipal Finance*, May 1961.

"Black Voices of the South." *Ebony*, August 1971.

Booth, E. J. R. "Interregional Income Differences." *Southern Economic Journal*, July 1964.

Borts, George. "The Estimation of Produced Income by State and Region." In *The Behavior of Income Shares*, National Bureau of Economic Research, Studies in Income and Wealth, vol. 27. New York: National Bureau of Economic Research, 1963.

Bradley, I. E. "Utah Interindustry Study." *Utah Economic and Business Review*, 1967.

Cobb, A. Lee. "Factors Affecting Industrial Location in Georgia." *Georgia Business*, May 1957.

Delwart, Louis, and Sidney Sonenblum. "Regional Account Projections in the Context of National Projections." In *Design of Regional Accounts*, edited by Werner Hochwald. Baltimore: The Johns Hopkins Press, 1961.

Denison, Edward F. "United States Economic Growth." *Journal of Business*, April 1962.

Easterlin, Richard D. "Interregional Differences in Per Capita Income, Population, and Total Income, United States, 1840-1959." In *Trends in the American Economy in the Nineteenth Century*, National Bureau of Economic Research, Studies in Income and Wealth, vol. 24. New York: National Bureau of Economic Research, 1960.

Fletcher, A. A. "When Industry Goes South." *Ebony*, August 1971.

Fromelt, E. John. "Gross State Product Estimates for South Dakota." *South Dakota Business Review*, May 1973.

Graham, Robert E., Jr. "The View from Washington." *Growth and Change*, April 1972.

Greenhut, Melvin L. "An Empirical Model and a Survey: New Plant Locations in Florida." *Review of Economics and Statistics*, November 1959.

Grubb, Herbert W., and William G. Lesso. "The Input-Output Model for the State of Texas." *Texas Business Review*, January 1974.

Hanna, Frank. "Analysis of Interstate Income Differentials—Theory and Practice." In *Regional Income*, National Bureau of Economic Research, Studies in Income and Wealth, vol. 21. Princeton, Princeton University Press, 1957.

Hirsch, Werner. "A General Structure for Regional Economic Analysis." In *Design of Regional Accounts*, edited by Werner Hochwald. Baltimore: The Johns Hopkins Press, 1961.

Hochwald, Werner. "Conceptual Issues in Regional Income Estimation." In *Regional Income*, National Bureau of Economic Research, Studies in Income and Wealth, vol. 21. Princeton: Princeton University Press, 1957.

Hughes, Rufus B., Jr. "Interregional Income Differences: Self Perpetuation." *Southern Economic Journal*, July 1961.

Isard, Walter. "Regional Commodity Balances and Interregional Commodity Flows." *American Economic Review*, May 1953.

————, and Guy Freutel. "Regional and National Product Projections and Their Interrelations." In *Long Range Economic Projections*, National Bureau of Economic Research, Studies in Income and Wealth, vol. 16. Princeton: Princeton University Press, 1954.

"It's Good to Be Home Again." *Ebony*, August 1971.

Kendrick, John W. "Productivity Trends: Capital and Labor," *Review of Economics and Statistics*, August 1956. (Also appeared as National Bureau of Economic Research, Occasional Paper No. 53, 1956.)

————, and C. Milton Jaycox. "The Concept and Estimation of Gross State Product." *Southern Economic Journal*, October 1965.

L'Esperance, W. L., G. Nestel, and D. Fromm. "Gross State Product and an Econometric Model of a State." *Journal of the American Statistical Association*, September 1969.

Leven, Charles. "Regional Income and Product Accounts: Construction and Applications." In *Design of Regional Accounts*, edited by Werner Hochwald. Baltimore: The Johns Hopkins Press, 1961.

Lynch, Gary A. "Estimating Idaho and Regional Gross Product." *Idaho Business and Economic Review*, June 1971.

McDonald, Stephen L. "On the South's Recent Economic Development." *Southern Economic Journal*, July 1961.

Meyer, John R. "Regional Economics: A Survey." *American Economic Review*, March 1963.

Mills, F. C. "The Role of Productivity in Economic Growth." *American Economic Review*, May 1952.

Moody, Harold T., Frank W. Puffer, and Robert M. Williams. "An Eight Region Model." *Growth and Change*, October 1970.

Moore, Frederick T., and James W. Petersen. "Regional Analysis: An Interindustry Model of Utah." *Review of Economics and Statistics*, November 1955.

Niemi, Albert W., Jr. "Georgia's Gross State Product." *Georgia Business*, October 1970.

Bibliography

———. "Georgia's Gross State Product, 1950-1971." *Georgia Business*, May 1973.

———. "A Re-Examination of the Kendrick-Jaycox Method of Estimating Gross State Product." *Review of Regional Studies*, Spring 1972.

Perloff, Harvey. "Problems of Assessing Regional Economic Progress." In *Regional Income*, National Bureau of Economic Research, Studies in Income and Wealth, vol. 21. Princeton: Princeton University Press, 1957.

Peterson, R. D., and R. A. Wykstra. "A Provisional Input-Output Study of Idaho's Economy." *University of Washington Business Review*, Winter 1968.

Ratajczak, Donald, and Robert M. Williams. "The Case for a Gross State Product Series." *Growth and Change*, April 1972.

Rice, Philip F., and R. Wayne Gober. "Lousiana Gross State Product." *The Lousiana Economy*, May 1973.

Ruggles, Richard, and Nancy Ruggles. "Regional Breakdowns of National Economic Accounts." In *Design of Regional Accounts*, edited by Werner Hochwald. Baltimore: The Johns Hopkins Press, 1961.

Sandoval, A. David. "A Development Strategy for New Mexico: 1961-1980." *New Mexico Business*. October 1970.

Schmookler, J. "Changing Efficiency of the American Economy, 1869-1938." *Review of Economics and Statistics*, August 1952.

Schultz, Theodore W. "Investment in Human Capital." *American Economic Review*, May 1960.

Solow, Robert M. "Technical Change and the Aggregate Production Function." *Review of Economics and Statistics*, August 1957.

Su, Teddy T. "A Note on Regional Input-Output Models." *Southern Economic Journal*, January 1970.

Tiebout, Charles M. "Exports and Regional Economic Growth." *Journal of Political Economy*, April 1956.

———. "Regional and Interregional Input-Output Models: An Appraisal." *Southern Economic Journal*, October 1957.

"White Voices of the South." *Ebony*, August 1971.

Williams, William V. "A Measure of the Impact of State and Local Taxes on Industry Location." *Journal of Regional Science*, Summer 1967.

GOVERNMENT PUBLICATIONS

Gottsegen, Jack J. "Revised Estimates of G.N.P. by Major Industries." *Survey of Current Business*, U.S. Department of Commerce, April 1967.

U.S. Bureau of the Census. *Annual Survey of Manufactures, 1950-1970.*

―――. *Census of Manufactures, 1954.*
―――. *Census of the United States: 1970, Detailed Characteristics, United States Summary.*
―――. *Statistical Abstract of the United States, 1950-1972.*
U.S. Department of Agriculture. *Agricultural Statistics, 1950-70.*
―――. *Farm Income Situation, Farm Income Supplement, 1971.*
U.S. Department of Commerce, *Personal Income by States since 1929,* 1955.
―――. *Survey of Current Business,* 1950-73.
U.S. Department of Labor. *Employment and Earnings Statistics for States and Areas, 1939-1970.*
U.S. Federal Power Commission. *All Electric Homes,* 1966.
―――. *Hydroelectric Power Resources of the United States,* 1972.

Index

A

Agglomeration effects, 52

Alabama: real output growth by major industry, 24-26; industrial composition of gross state product, 27; industry shares of national output, 28; labor productivity growth, 29-31; per capita output levels, 32; per capita output growth, 32-33; per capita output relatives, 34-35; per capita output trends relative to national average, 38-39; per capita output trends relative to Southeast average, 40-41; role of productivity in real output growth, 46; role of productivity in per capita output growth, 47; role of manufacturing in growth, 49; per capita income growth relative to national average, 53; unionization, 55; failure rate on Armed Forces Qualifications test, 57

Arizona: input-output, 7

Arkansas: real output growth by major industry, 24-26; industrial composition of gross state product, 27; industry shares of national output, 28-29; labor productivity growth, 29-31; per capita output levels, 32; per capita output growth, 32-33; per capita output relatives, 34-35; per capita output trends relative to national average, 37-39; per capita output trends relative to Southeast average, 40-41; role of productivity in real output growth, 46; role of productivity in per capita output growth, 47; role of manufacturing in growth, 49; per capita income growth relative to national average, 53; unionization, 55; failure rate on Armed Forces Qualifications Test, 57

Armed Forces Qualifications Test: failure rate, 57

B

Bank of California, 8

Bergin, Thomas, 51

Booth, E. J. R., 36

C

Capital. See Industrial location

Charlesworth, Harold K., 5, 8

Charlesworth-Herzel estimation procedure, 6

Climate. See Industrial location

Colberg, Marshall R., 58

Coleman Report, 57-58; Interpretation of results, 105n

D

Data problems, state and regional, 3, 8, 14, 20

Deflation, 12-13

Deflators, implicit industry, 12

Denison, Edward, 43

Dunn, Edgar, 50

E

Eagan, William, 51

Earnings: South relative to national average, by major occupation, 55-56

Econometric models: University of California at Los Angeles and University of Pennsylvania, 8

Economic accounts, state, 7

Education: role in economic growth, 43; low quality in South, 57

Educational attainment: median years of completed educaton, U.S. and South, 56-57

Efficiency. See Productivity

F

Factor proportions, 11, 14

Factor substitution, 20; in productivity growth, 43, 102n, 104n. See also Productivity increment

116